PRISONER
OF
WOODSTOCK

PRISONER
OF
WOODSTOCK

Dallas Taylor

THUNDER'S MOUTH PRESS • NEW YORK

Copyright © 1994 by Dallas Taylor
All rights reserved

First edition
First printing, 1994

Published by
Thunder's Mouth Press
632 Broadway, 7th Floor
New York, NY 10012

Library of Congress Cataloging-in-Publication Data

Taylor, Dallas.
    Prisoner of Woodstock / Dallas Taylor. — 1st ed.
      p. cm.
    Includes index.
    ISBN 1-56025-072-0 : $22.95
    1. Taylor, Dallas.   2. Rock musicians — United States — Biography.
ML419.T22A3   1994
781.66'092 — dc20   93-46075
[B]   CIP
                                                    MN

Printed in the United States of America
Design by Bernard Schleifer
Typeset by AeroType, Inc.

Distributed by
Publishers Group West
4065 Hollis Street
Emeryville, CA 94608
(800) 788-3123

DEDICATION

For Betty, Dallas Troy, Sharlotte, Michael, Stephen, Jeannie,
Troy Taylor, Sr., Violet Cantu, and my sister Darlene

David, Stephen, Graham, and Neil
Without you there would be no story . . .

Teach your children well
Their father's hell
Did slowly go by.
And feed them on your dreams . . .

CONTENTS

INTRODUCTIONS

ACKNOWLEDGMENTS

1	Whoopie, We're All Going to Die	3
2	The Suicide Attempt	27
3	Safety in Numbers	43
4	The Awakening	63
5	Wish Upon a Star	81
6	The Christmas Tree	107
7	The Prison	149
8	The Party	171
9	The Clock	197
10	Reunion	209
11	The Circle Closes	227
	EPILOGUE	237
	INDEX	239

Introductions

Every year since I started playing music in Los Angeles, I have watched the young, aspiring and often talented kids wander into the scene here and try to get a start. Some of them get lucky, but most of them are just cannon fodder. They are grist for the mill of "The Business." It's sad, you know, because they arrive believing that music is magic and that it will set them free. Of course, the "music is magic" side and the music business are diametrically opposed, and the business winds up eating these kids alive.

As a matter of fact, there are a whole list of mistakes, peripheral traps that pull you away from the central, and only important concern — music. Money, glory, fame, sex, adulation, peer group approval, competition and one's own emotional baggage all distract you from your original purpose.

As far as I know, Dallas didn't miss any of these mistakes. They crept up on him, and jerked the rug out from under him, and derailed him and almost killed him.

Why he and I are alive when Janis and Jimi and Cass and . . . and . . . well that list is too long and way too painful. I don't know why we're alive, except we had what the French call *raison d'être*, a reason for being—music. We also found the love of great women. We also went to a lot of meetings. I think someone else helped, too.

I use Dallas as an example when I'm speaking to people about surviving the drug experience. I think he has wound up being a hell of a good example.

I know he's wound up being a hell of a good friend.

—David Crosby

I first met Dallas in 1968 when I was recording the song "Red Eye Express" with John Sebastian who was taking a hiatus from his band The Lovin' Spoonful. I had been introduced to John by my great friend Cass Elliott. It seems that most of the people that had a good influence on me were brought into my life by Cass. Dallas Taylor was no exception. Here was a fine drummer, a musician with great touch, great feel and a quiet sense of humor. This last quality was to stand him in good stead as our years together went screaming by.

Broken dreams, fading memories, but always the look on Dallas's face when he laughed, the face of a child, the face of Dallas Jr. Dallas trusted me and I liked that. As Stephen and David and I were getting that first record together, Big D was there. He was our compadre, our drummer, part of our family. We knew what we had and took great pleasure in sharing our music with anyone that would listen, and listen they did to those harmonies that had thrilled the three of us from that beginning verse. We can't remember for certain exactly where it was that our sound was first born. David and I believe that it was in Joni's living room in Laurel Canyon, Stephen thinks that it took place in Cass's kitchen up on Mulholland Drive. Perhaps Dallas knows.

Dallas and I took up lodging in Stephen's house in the valley in the spring of '69 and we did what every other band did, stayed up all night playing, staying high and getting better at our craft. We shared our lives, our drugs and our hearts. Dallas would share with me his hopes and dreams and stories of his pilot father who crashed and burned too young. I remember looking back at him when we were on stage at Woodstock and thinking that me and him weren't so different. We came from similar economic backgrounds and had shared the fact that we both had lost our fathers too soon. In a way the music festival at Max Yasgur's farm became the sort of myth that was far greater in its impact than the real show was. Yes, hundreds of thousands of people had come to the farm, some interesting music had been made, some reputations had grown larger but in reality it was miserably wet, muddy and tremendously exciting all at the same time. I guess Crosby, Stills and Nash were remembered as one of the best new acts because up until that show very few people had ever seen us even though our record was at the top of the carts. We had made it big time and so had Dallas.

After the thrills of becoming successful with our music we drifted apart and I heard that Dallas also crashed and burned like his father before him. Maybe he couldn't face the future without being in the band, maybe he had his own devils that were tormenting him. During his bad times I heard that he lived close to me when I was married to Susan but we never did run into each other, probably lived at separate ends of the day. I thought of him often but didn't seek him out. Later on he told me that he had been in a sort of a jail, somewhere that he could not escape from. He had been a prisoner, a prisoner of Woodstock.

—Graham Nash

Acknowledgments

The author would like to thank the following for their undying support

Eric and Janis Gardner
Jan Miller and staff at Dupree-Miller
Neil Ortenberg, Rebecca Corris, and
Joseph Mills at Thunder's Mouth Press
Joan Fucillo

George Blair, M.D.
Gary Gitnick, M.D.
Michela Gunn, M.D.
Todd Howard, M.D.
Leonard Makowka, M.D.
David Murphy, M.D.
Maxine Ostrum, M.D.
Luis Podesta, M.D.
Stephen Shea, M.D.
Linda Sher, M.D.
Thomas Trott, M.D.

Gregory Allman
Tom and Roseanne Arnold
David Bender
Richard Block
Bobaloo
Jeannie Bray
Cedars-Sinai Transplant team 1990
Jimmy Caan
Lori Cerasoli
Tita Cheney
Jan Crosby
Lori Davis
Henry Diltz
Jean Firstenberg
Friends at Exodus and Behavioral Health - Daniel Freeman Marina Hospital
John Good and Drum Workshop Staff
Todd Gold
Guys from Monday night meeting
Newt Harrell
Richie and Deborah Hayward
Alan Henderson
Steve Hochman
Peter Hyams
Rob and Sheryl Lowe
Michael Morris and Zildjian Cymbals
Luana Murphy
Susan Nash
Michael and Diana Nathanson
Judd Nelson
Robin Newton
Neal Preston

Paul A. Rothchild
Nikki Sixx
Richard and Barbara Starkey
Troy Taylor
Bob Timmins
Paul and Polly Tobias
Ugly Brothers
Veince band members
Fred and Westwood Music
Bill Wilson
Rosalind Wyman
Robert Wyman and Peggy Giffin
Brad and Leza Ann Wyman

1

Whoopie, We're All Going to Die

"Who brought the Pop Tarts?"

"I can't find that Guns N' Roses tape," someone else says, nervously.

"We're opening and closing with Crosby, Stills, Nash, and Young," someone replies.

"Who are they?" a young voice asks.

I turn to give her a nasty look, but can't pick her out of the crowd of people in green surgical gowns gathered around me.

"Don't think about it, Dad," my son says, squeezing my hand. In this sea of antiseptic green confusion he is my only anchor, and for a few seconds his presence calms me down. I fix on his eyes, which are also mine and my mother's, and fight off the urge to let in the past. Letting in the memories now would be too close to seeing my life flash before my eyes and I want no jinxing of the next twelve hours.

"Where are the potato chips?" a voice calls from another room.

"Is this a fucking picnic or an operating room?" I demand, expecting everyone to drop everything and apologize. But they ignore me and continue with their work, moving, adjusting, and testing equipment.

I lie on a hard table in the middle of the room, trussed like a turkey waiting to be carved. This is a liver transplant — my liver. I think about what that means, a *trans*plant. Something alive is being pulled from its soil in the hope it will take root in mine. Cutting and scraping and digging and filling the hole with a liver accustomed to detoxifying another life. I am filled with absurd notions. . . . What if it doesn't like the things I like to eat? What if it's used to chicken pot pie or borscht or whale blubber? Maybe it will be angry or morose at not being able to die with its spleen and gall bladder and everything else it knows. Do I want a depressed or pissed-off organ inside me? And maybe, just maybe, the doctors are wrong and the itching and bleeding and bloating and forgetfulness and lethargy are all caused by a virus or anxiety or turning forty-two. They could have mixed up my tests and scans with someone else's; it happens all the time. Maybe these fucking doctors are looking for a guinea pig or a downpayment on a new Mercedes. This train of thought is not new and it is silly but it worries me nonetheless. So I focus on my son, but I can't help saying, "I wonder whose it is?" He smiles and immediately changes the subject. It is too sad to think that someone's dying has given me this chance.

The anesthesiologist, one of the major players in this game, is a small, quick man with wild eyes above his mask and curly hair below his cap. He looks way too much like Harpo Marx.

Harpo finishes checking his equipment and puts his face too close to mine.

"All set?" he asks.

I'm certain he has a wooden mallet hidden under his scrubs.

"I've changed my mind," I say, half seriously.

"Count back from one hundred," he says while injecting something into my IV bag.

"Once this is over, Pop, it'll be great. You'll have a new life," my son says as he gives my hand another squeeze. "You'll be able to do anything—the sky's the limit."

I start counting and watch the IV bag as it begins draining into my arm. At ninety-seven I feel a warm, familiar feeling that I haven't felt since I got sober five years ago. My first instinct is to feel guilty and to resist, because the quest for this feeling is the very reason I'm here on this table. But at ninety-five the seduction is too strong and I feel myself floating and now there is no resisting the flood of the past.

"This'll take us just a minute," said the helicopter pilot as he punched at his controls and jerked us up into the air. "Make yourselves comfortable."

The helicopter was loud, small and windy, not at all conducive to conversation or drug use. Nevertheless, I tried both—pulling a coke vial out of my pocket and turning to talk to Graham Nash. Graham responded with a tolerant smile. I hated tolerant smiles, even from people I liked, and especially from Graham, whom I looked up to. Graham had just left the Hollies and joined our band. He was educated, polite, and eloquent. He possessed an ability to charm and steal women from his friends the likes of which I'd never before seen. Graham's leaving was devastating to the Hollies. He'd written most of their big hits, although they wrote "He's Not

Heavy, He's My Brother" about Graham's leaving them for CSN. Graham seemed so superior to me in every way that at times I felt I should pay him for letting me tag along.

Somehow though, cocaine made me feel this less keenly. Coke was the "great equalizer," making me feel less terrified of saying or doing the wrong thing, making possible an almost natural interaction with someone like Graham. It was, however, damned difficult to get the stuff up your nose in a helicopter.

"This music worth all this fuss?" asked the pilot.

With my coke vial crammed up my nose and my head craned back so far I was staring at the floor behind my seat, I said, "It's the dawn of a new day." I'd heard someone, somewhere, say that and it sounded good, so I said it whenever anyone asked me any question relating even vaguely to Woodstock. I felt another of Graham's tolerant smiles trained on me and it raised my body temperature ten degrees. Yet of the two of us, it was Graham who probably truly believed that this festival was the beginning of a new day; that peace and free love and social sanity would come, inevitably conquering modern man's need to acquire, dominate, and discriminate. And that new day would dawn to the strains of Crosby, Stills, Nash and Young's next album. As for me, I really didn't care. Oh, of course I said I did, and I definitely saw myself as part of the solution. But to be honest, I cared more about Ferraris and drugs and poking any cute blond thing who wanted to touch a rock star. My real goal was to have all three at once on the Ventura Freeway while doing 85 on the way to Malibu. Richard Nixon was an irrelevant, ridiculous-looking anachronism who simply missed the point; the Military-Industrial Complex was as unfathomable as all of the income tax forms that my accountant had started shoving into my face. Irreverence, irresponsibility, and self-destructiveness were required to be a rock star and I was ready to give it my all.

"Any further and you'll suck that thing into your lung," Graham said. The helicopter suddenly jerked up and down.

"Wind currents," said the pilot, who appeared to be enjoying them, as well as my terror, entirely too much. I hated heights. My father had been an airshow stunt pilot and at one time all I'd wanted was to fly, too, but the whole thing had soured for me, and I could no longer enjoy the experience.

"Can this thing go any slower?" I asked, searching for my vial.

"Not without pitching into the ground," said the pilot with a smile. "You guys famous?"

Our first album was out and headed toward number one but we didn't have much of a following yet. People knew Stephen Stills from Buffalo Springfield, David Crosby from the Byrds, and Graham from the Hollies, and they sometimes recognized me as the person on the back of the album cover, peering out through the screen door, but this was only our second live performance. We were sloppy and inexperienced, a band composed of fairly talented musicians hampered by enormous egos and the consequent belief that rehearsal was for amateurs. Tonight we were going to perform in front of half a million people and every rock critic in the universe—armed only with a great deal of cocaine and the firmly held belief that the magic of the moment would carry us through.

"Not yet," I told the pilot. "But tomorrow we will be."

"What's the name of your band?" he asked.

"What's the name of that lake down there?" I responded. His question made me uncomfortable. I was a founding member of the band and yet my name wasn't part of its title. Neil Young was about to join and his last name would be included. I understood the argument—he was famous and wouldn't join otherwise. Still, I was hurt and insulted and any time the question came up, something twisted sharp and deep in my gut.

"That ain't no lake," said the pilot, laughing at us. "That's your audience. That's Woodstock."

The crowd below exactly resembled a large, choppy lake set in the middle of rolling green hills and fed by a hundred streams. Shining miniature cars clogged the roads in all directions for as far as I could see.

Losing his cool for once, Graham actually screamed. "Quite a crowd!"

"The fucking dawn of a new day!" I said to myself as the panic started taking over.

I hated crowds. I was always afraid that people would finally discover that I was the no-talent average-looking ass-hole that only my soon-to-be-ex-wife and I knew I was. I'm too short and dark, with a potbelly and my father's peculiar first name, which always got me into fights with anyone who thought it clever to call me "Lubbock" or "Abilene."

I looked over at Graham, who seemed to have it all, and I found myself thinking of the time when I was ten, and the eleven year old I was in love with rejected me because my eyebrows were too bushy. I'll bet Graham never had a minute of that, I thought. Whereas I've always needed to have an edge, an ace in the hole. When my mother took me to see a movie about Gene Krupa, I discovered my ace: I was going to be a famous drummer.

That was in 1958, when rock & roll was very young. I was only ten, and I was absolutely hooked. My sister, Darlene, dark, Annette Funicello-like, and twelve years older, loaned me albums: Roy Orbison, Elvis, Fats Domino, Little Richard, the Ventures. I worked loading a crop duster for a man named Fricke to get the money to buy a set of drums. He was tall and blond with an enormous cleft in his chin. He really didn't need the help, but he was an old family friend and a nice man. I liked working for him because I needed those drums, and I also liked having a father. My parents had divorced when I was six and my own father lived out in Phoenix with his new wife, Jeannie, a wonderful woman who I really cared about.

After Fricke finished a day of dusting the field, he'd come visit with my mother and me and we'd sit on the front porch swing or on the swing under the willow tree behind the house, then they would go into town for dancing or a movie. We lived in a white clapboard house in San Antonio with my grandparents and my uncles, so I slept in the same room as my mother. When she'd come home late from one of these dates, humming and sometimes stumbling into things, I would pretend I was asleep. She would undress silently and slip into bed with one, quick motion and within a very few minutes her breathing would become deep and regular and calming. She slept with a piece of bread underneath her pillow because someone told her it was the best way to deal with choking in the middle of the night, and she would never sleep on her left side because she didn't like to hear the sound of her own heartbeat. When I was little, I slept next to her, and I couldn't fall asleep at night unless I could twirl my fingers in her hair. When I was six and a half, my father said I was too old to be sharing her bed, so my grandfather brought up a cot from the basement. I had trouble falling asleep for months.

One awful night we heard the news that Fricke had been killed when his crop duster hit a power pole. I wanted to break my father's rule and sleep next to my mother, but she silently led me back to my cot and as quickly as ever she slid into bed and turned out the lights. I waited for her deep breathing and its calming effect on me but it didn't come. I, too, lay awake all night. I was trying to remember what Fricke's teeth looked like. The radio had reported that they had been dug out of the instrument panel of his plane and I wanted to remember his smile. My mother had always seemed kind of quiet and sad to me and after Fricke died she became even quieter and sadder.

But I got my drums and my mother arranged for me to take lessons with Mr. Hart. He was a small, old man with a mustache and both he and his chubby wife treated me like their prodigy grandchild. Mr. Hart's studio was small and dingy, filled with worn and torn drums, a xylophone, and an intriguing pile of unidentifiable percussion instruments. I was so enthusiastic that I quickly became impatient with my progress. Probably fearing that my impatience would soon turn into disinterest, at the end of one session Mr. Hart handed me an album: *Music Minus One.* It was one in a series of records which were basically instrumental versions of all kinds of songs, but lacking the drum part—which I was to provide. I played along with hits by the Everly Brothers, the Ventures, and Chuck Berry, and after less than a year of lessons and obsessive practice, my mother went out and got me an agent.

Herbie Cohen was soft and moist, a middle-aged man who wore bad shirts. Easily convinced by my mother that I was better than Buddy Rich and that my youth would prove an asset rather than a liability, he immediately began getting me bookings. The first was with a Drum and Bugle Corps for a Thanksgiving Day Parade. We marched flanked by thirty baton twirlers. Herbie only dimly understood my resistance to a repeat booking at Christmas. Then my mother convinced him that there would be no legal problems with a twelve year old playing in night clubs as long as she accompanied me, so Herbie started getting me gigs with bands that played at Army and Air Force bases. Sporting a thin-lapeled blazer and clip-on tie, I played with country & western bands, polka and swing ensembles, and lounge combos all over Texas. My mother would sit at the front table watching me silently through the haze of cigarette smoke and diffuse neon lighting, as every male in the room, including Herbie, watched her. She was very pretty, with hazel eyes, deeply tanned skin, and long platinum-dyed hair pulled away from her face, falling softly over her shoulders.

"Here we go," the pilot said.

The landing pad was a dusty blemish of dirt in a littered, orange field just on the fringe of the tents and Winnebagos that were set up for the performers and their people. We were descending quickly. Far below I could see a lone figure madly waving us in with a tie-dyed shirt. At about fifty feet I recognized the running, jumping person as John Sebastian and guessed that his dance was due more to some strong leafy substance in his system than to some overwhelming desire for us to land. John and I were good friends. In fact, he was responsible for my being a member of CSN in the first place. John loved me, and was hurt that CSN had stolen me from his band.

At forty feet the engine jerked, heaved, coughed, quit, and the helicopter started plummeting to the ground.

"Oh, oh," said the pilot.

"What do you mean, 'Oh, oh'?" I yelled, suddenly more alert than I'd been in three years. Graham went white. The pilot kicked at the control panel and I searched my memory for any prayer dealing with redemption. When nothing religious came to mind, I seized upon the first secular equivalent available to me.

"I'm sorry!" I screamed over and over, louder and louder hoping to drown out the sounds of breaking glass, metal, and bones that would come at any second. At the height of my hysteria, I looked over to Graham, expecting to see some reflection of my own terror. I saw only that same look of superiority—perhaps it had been frozen on— and I lifted my leg as high into the air as I could under the circumstances and resolved that my last earthly act would be kicking in a smug, English face. I had just taken aim, when suddenly the control panel responded to the pilot's kicking, and the engine choked and whirred into action. We jerked upward a quick hundred feet; my foot was slammed to the floor and a whiplash that would have snapped the spine of a sober man turned Graham's smile into a grimace. Delighted with the turn of events, and with the fact that I hadn't made any promises or resolutions so I didn't have to worry about divine retribution when I didn't keep them, I shook Graham's hand and stuck my face up to the window to watch our landing. I saw that John was still dancing below.

"Wow, man, are you guys OK?" John asked as we climbed out of the helicopter.

"Just fucking great!" I said. "Remind me never to fly in one of those things again."

If ever there was a person who deserved to be rich, famous and adored by millions, it was John Sebastian. Kind, unassuming, unreasonably friendly and forgiving, he was also truly talented.

"What's happening?" I asked, screaming over the noise of the chopper engine.'

"Oh, what isn't?" he said. He motioned for me to follow him and we headed for the tents behind the stage.

The day was warm and muggy with a feel of rain. The heavy air smelled of unwashed women, cheap wine, and pot and the ground was wet and thick with mud, but no one seemed to notice or mind. The crowd beyond the stage was deafening, larger than any I'd ever seen; the crowd behind the stage was smaller, but just as impressive. Hundreds of wives, girlfriends and groupies of every imaginable size, shape and tie-dyed configuration were streaming in and out of hundreds of tents and makeshift cabins and Winnebagos. All were swaying vaguely to the rhythm that came from the stage, and all were keeping an eye open for a famous piece of ass. Sex charged the air and that thrill, that electricity, like cocaine, made everything vivid and personal and promising. Graham followed me following John and we wound our way through what seemed like gaggles and prides of groupies, girls with firm, round, barely touched and hardly clad breasts and bellies and hips. Every few feet we were stopped for handshakes, kisses, and hits off joints and finally we made it to John's tent and some rather extraordinary hashish. Country Joe McDonald was singing "Whoopie, We're All Going to Die!" as we sat down and started our first serious drug abuse of the day.

"When are you guys on?" John asked, as he took a very long hit from the hash pipe.

"Ask Stills," Graham said. Stephen was the business-man, the planner, and the organizer, and he had arrived by helicopter before us to plan, to organize, and undoubtedly to plunder.

"Figure out the best time to go on stage and you've figured out what Stills and Geffen have booked us for," I said, grabbing for the pipe.

"God bless ambition," John said smiling. "Are you ready?"

"For stardom, not for an audience," I said.

"Smells good," Graham said, reaching for the pipe and eyeing the dark-haired teenage girl he was sitting next to. The girl was just sober enough to see that her breasts were falling out of her too-small top, but not sober enough to do anything about it. "The audience means nothing," he said.

John completely understood Graham's grandiosity. He knew that our band wasn't really ready to perform, but he also intimately knew all of the egos involved.

"Anyone know if Neil's around?" he asked.

"He's here somewhere," I said. "He'll be on with us for the electric set but won't be playing on the acoustic set. He's got a lot going on and I think he's still unsure about adding his 'Y' to our shingle. You know, the man keeps to himself."

John smiled, lifted his guitar and started to tune up. At that moment Jerry Garcia poked his head through the tent flaps.

"Wow, man!" he said, starting to clap. "Hippie rock stars! Will you guys autograph my butt?"

"No thanks," Graham answered, without taking his eyes off the nearly comatose teenager.

"Heavy, man," Jerry said, before someone pulled him out of the tent and back into the stream of people winding its way through the camp. I had never met Jerry Garcia before and was more than a little surprised and impressed, but of course I didn't let on.

"Who was that?" I asked in my most indifferent Graham Nash-like voice.

"Nobody," said Graham still intent on the untended breasts. "Nobody."

The hash started washing away my fear of the crowd. John finished tuning his guitar and started singing softly. Faces popped in and out of the tent and I laid back on a stack of pillows and watched John sing about rainbows and love all over my blues.

John was like a big brother to me and he was responsible for my being here. I'd met him one afternoon more than a year ago, while I was practicing at Elektra Records' studios. Paul Rothchild, who had produced me when I was playing with a band called Clear Light, was there producing John's solo album and he arranged for John to hear me play. Clear Light was kind of a bizarre psychedelic Grateful Dead-type band. When we were good, we were really good. But most of the time we stunk. Anyway, John liked what he heard when I played for him, and he asked me to join him on the album. He was very big then and I remember how amazingly unaffected he was, and how good he made me feel about myself. His first solo album was only a modest success but the record company wanted a second one, so he asked me to play with him again. It was winter and John invited me to his house in Sag Harbor, Long Island, for some rehearsals. He'd also invited some old friends—Stephen Stills, Graham Nash and David Crosby—for advice, moral support, and background vocals, and it was during these rehearsals that they asked me to join a new band that they were forming. They had originally planned on keeping the band acoustic and focusing exclusively on their harmonies, but when they heard me play they knew that drums could punctuate their music without dominating it, so they called up their managers, David Geffen and Elliot Roberts, and I was in.

Still, in some ways, I felt I had to constantly prove myself to them, especially to Graham, who was lukewarm about having me in the group. His musical solution for the future included only acoustical back-up for his lighter-than-air harmonies, though lately he'd become more accepting. Somehow, I felt that his initial uneasiness was similar to my grandmother's misgivings when she'd heard I was going to take up the drums; she said there was something dark and dirty about pumping and thumping on animal skins, which shouldn't be encouraged. David was more enthusiastic but by far, Stephen was the most responsive. We had hit it off right away. Maybe that had something to do with the fact that we were both from Texas, but he was especially sensitive to percussion and was probably the only one who considered me essential rather than just backup.

I loved playing with him. Everything was about feeling and action and reaction. He was aggressive and impulsive and impatient and always wanted to experiment and push the limits. Playing with him was like dancing with someone who always surprised you with a new step or twist. You were forced to move quickly and if you didn't respond with something equally innovative he'd get bored and look for another partner on the stage. The constant push and pull, leading and following made for terrifically creative sessions. When I was behind my drums we were partners and equals. I was calm and happy, all of my insecurities went.

Then at one point that winter Graham looked at me and said, "We'll always take care of you kid," and I believed it would be all right. It was around Christmas, and we were all living in Sag Harbor just down the road from John, in an A-frame house Stephen had rented for us. We were working and David Geffen was ironing out the details of the contract with Ahmet Ertegun and Atlantic Records. One day when Geffen was at the house, he and Stephen and David were talking in one of the bedrooms. They had made it clear that it wasn't something they wanted me to hear and I was starting to get that sinking feeling of being left out. Then Geffen called Graham over and I followed, but when we got to the door Stephen said, "D—could you please excuse us a minute? We're talking some business." Geffen was brusque, telling me to go back to staring at the cracks in the wall while I waited for them.

From what I could tell, Geffen was saying it was a bad idea to ask me to join the band.

"The guy's a goon. You could get any drummer and pay him scale."

But Stephen knew there was something magic when we played together and Stephen was the leader, so what Stephen wanted, Stephen got. Then Stephen insisted that my picture be on the album cover and Geffen really got angry.

"We've already taken the cover shots. And why give up points to that country bumpkin?"

"I don't give a fuck! Take a picture of him and put it on the back or something!" said Stephen. Then they just looked at each other.

Actually, I think that Geffen's dislike of me was, at least partly, personal. I was sleeping with Laura Nyro then and Geffen knew it. He was her manager, and I think they had even had a thing going at one time. Also, Laura had written a song about me, which is kind of an honor. I liked that. I'm sure he didn't.

Stephen was on top then, so I felt protected. No one would seriously mess with me, even though I had no written contract. It was all done with handshakes. Barely a year later, that was starting to change. The cocaine had become more and more a part of our lives—at one point we had even thought of calling our group the Frozen Noses—and I watched Stephen slowly losing control. Some nights through my drug-hazed sleep, I'd hear Stephen calling me, "Wake up D! I got this new song and we've got to get it on tape!"

I'd manage to get semiconscious enough to say, "What, man, it's three A.M. I'm too fucking out of it. Let me sleep."

Then Stephen would start shoving a small gold spoon in my nose saying, "Here, this'll wake you up." I'd take a long, deep sniff, the blood would rush through my veins and I'd wake up.

"Let's rock and roll!"

When we first got together that winter in Sag Harbor, there was talk of John joining, too, but gradually this died down. John's wife, Laurie, had convinced him that it would be a bad business move, that he was more successful than any of us. I later learned it was because Graham was sleeping with Laurie. I was still just a kid from Texas where sleeping with a friend's wife was wrong, regardless of what drug you were on, and I really felt that John should have kicked the shit out of Graham every time he saw him, not hug him, sing and pass him a joint. But I could never bring myself to talk to Graham about it and I wasn't sure whether John knew. Anyway, whenever we were together my anger and indignation would be diffused by a noseful or lungful of something illegal. And I soon discovered that my thinking was wrong, or at least misguided. These guys were all older than I was and had seen much more of the world; they had much more education and had done many more drugs. They were clearly more enlightened, and were at the forefront of a generational upheaval that was going to change society completely. The best thing for me to do would be to keep my hang-ups to myself until time and drugs worked their magic and I, too, achieved that level of greater understanding. But every time we played "Lady of the Island," a song written by Graham about Laurie, I had to fight off a very powerful urge to sit John down and tell him all about it.

"This sucks!" shouted Stephen as he burst into the tent.

"Mellow out," said David, entering right behind him. They wore expensive jackets and looked conspicuously clean and dry and rich.

"Someone fucked up. What the hell do Geffen and Roberts do for their money? I'm not paying them for this kind of shit."

"Hey, man," said John, "it's a party."

"It ain't a fucking party when the entertainment starts after everyone's gone to bed. We're scheduled to go on 'sometime around midnight'," Stephen said.

"Man, no one is going to be sleeping out there. This is a happening! A gigantic love-in! This is an all-night party!" said David.

"Let's begin the set with a drum solo," I said. "I'll pump those fucking skins so hard no one will be asleep for miles. I'll wake the goddamn dead."

"It's insulting," said Stephen. "And that ain't the worst of it. Hendrix is getting paid three times what we're getting."

Graham's comatose teenager came alive at the mention of Jimi Hendrix's name, and Graham stiffened. Jimi was a star and that rubbed Graham the wrong way. The mention of

21

Hendrix's name rubbed me the wrong way too, but for different reasons. I'd first met Hendrix a couple of years earlier at a club in New York called Steve Paul's Scene. My band, Clear Light, had been playing on a bill with the Doors and through Jim Morrison I met a beautiful Spanish hooker named Denise. She had been sleeping with Morrison, but she soon dropped him for me. I was married, but I saw Denise whenever I could and I was with her at the Scene the night Hendrix arrived fresh from England with his new band, the Experience. Denise said this guy was going to be the next sex symbol of rock & roll—and she was right. Not long afterwards, Denise called late one night inviting me over. When I arrived the door was opened by Hendrix who stood there stark naked, insisting that I come in. I was one of his biggest fans but I was a little reluctant to take him up on it. Finally, I went in and Denise joined us from another room. She was also naked. They invited me to leave my clothes on the floor and join them in some sex and drugs. I thanked them but declined, giving some wife- or child-related excuse, and exited a little too quickly to appear nonchalant. Since then I had avoided them both but I felt bad about it. Clearly, one of my hang-ups was getting in the way. I also felt bad about being second fiddle. After all, Denise dropped me for Hendrix who wrote the song "Gypsy Eyes" for her—although she had started sleeping with me again since I had joined CSN. A true groupie.

"What are we getting paid?" I asked. The blanket of serenity that had covered the room a few minutes ago had been torn to shreds. John put down his guitar and joined me on the pillows. I pulled a joint out of my pocket and waved it in his direction but he resisted, smiling. The real world was creeping into his ideal one and the battle looked unwinnable.

"The money isn't the point, man. You know that, Stephen," John said.

"Baez, Creedence Clearwater Revival, Airplane, Joplin, the Band—they're all making more than us. Fucking Canned Heat is making more than we are!" said Stephen.

"They won't be after tonight," said Graham, suddenly interested in the conversation. "We blow them away tonight—we name our price." The room grew silent, and for the first time I saw fear on Stephen's face. Failure was a possibility, however unlikely.

"Think good thoughts, and lose the Los Angeles jackets," John said. "Get wet and pretend you're one of them."

"This is our time!" said David.

"There are men on the moon!" I said. "Even the sky ain't a fucking limit anymore."

Stephen brightened. He stopped pacing and sat down with us and I lit the joint and began passing it around. From the other direction came cheap California white wine and expensive and very pure cocaine. John smiled and put his arm around me and I wished that I found the sunshine that followed him around as alluring as the dark clouds that were certainly gathering.

For a second I flashed on Herbie and my mother. Until now, I had very bad luck with bands when I picked them myself. Like I said, I went looking for black clouds to sit under—or maybe one really did follow me around. Herbie and my mother had always chosen my gigs for me, but after a year I'd had it with playing the top forty at a respectable volume. I was thirteen when Mac Ray and the Invictas asked me to join them. They were all older than me and they were cool enough to name themselves after an automobile. So I extricated myself from something Herbie had arranged and joined them. We played all over South Texas at dances and clubs and Bar Mitzvahs, anyplace that was willing to take a chance on six teenagers who were striving to take the music of the Ventures one step closer to the edge. I'd been with them for about a year when my mother died and my father took me to Arizona. Six months later I ran away, hitchhiking across New Mexico and back home to Texas. Somehow, I'd managed to arrive in San Antonio an hour before the band was heading south for a one-night stand, so I borrowed some drums and joined them. I remember that while we were playing I felt safe, happy to be with the only family I felt I had.

On the ride home that night, I sat in the back of the red Comet with three other players while our guitarist, Peter, drove and our keyboard player, Augie, sat in the passenger's seat. It was two in the morning, raining and slippery but we felt secure, weighted to the road by the trailer full of instruments hooked onto the car. I fell asleep, then I awoke to a tearing sound and shrieks and the sight of the hood ornament of the oncoming car that was ripping ours in half. A drunk driver had fallen asleep at the wheel and swerved into us, killing Peter instantly. The rest of us were cut from the car with acetylene torches and taken to intensive care units.

Of all of us Augie was the most badly damaged: he was paralyzed from the neck down. I was lucky — my neck was broken, but there wasn't any spinal cord or nerve damage. But with my nervous system intact I could feel the pain of my punctured lung, broken shoulder, and my belly swelling from internal bleeding. There were some terrible days ahead. My father showed up two weeks later and discharged me from the ICU to take me back to Arizona and a "normal life." I agreed that the accident was a sign that I should change my path, and

I promised to start attending school again. As soon as I was well enough to get out of bed, I ran away.

A second sign came three years later, almost to the minute. I was seventeen, married, and playing with my new Texas band. We were in Scottsdale, Arizona, in the parking lot of a nightclub, packing up our instruments to go home after a successful gig. It was very late at night. Everyone had already left but the bass player, Walter, and me. Walter was a great guy with a thick drawl and a good sense of humor. He wore glasses and, like me, he had a wife and kid. Then five guys with buzz haircuts, white dress shirts, and dark slacks—what today we would call preppies—started making fun of the length of our hair. Walter was the kind of guy who had a long fuse, so we ignored the calls of "faggots" and "sissies" and finished packing up the car. We were driving out of the parking lot when we heard a loud smash. The beer bottle broke on the windshield of my Mustang. Within a second, Walter was out of the car.

"Shit!" I yelled, realizing I would have to get out and help Walter and that, given the numbers, we were probably going to be beaten up pretty badly. I reached under the front seat and took out a razor blade that I kept for such emergencies and joined him. By the time I got out of the car, three of these drunk rich kids were all over Walter. They had him down on the ground and were punching and kicking him in the chest and head. As I ran over to him, I was jumped by the other two guys, who were not quite as big but who were wielding beer bottles. Turning and twisting, I sank the razor into one of them and cut him open from armpit to waistline. He jumped back, not realizing what had happened. When he looked down and saw the blood, he started to scream. The noise brought out the manager of the club who had already called the police. He came running over to break us up. The guys ran off and I went

25

to Walter, who couldn't lift himself from the ground. He was bleeding from the mouth and nose and was slurring his words. The manager wanted me to wait for the police but I put Walter in the car and drove him to the hospital.

In the emergency room the doctor applied bandages and ice and said nothing was wrong, that Walter would get over the headache, the slurred speech, and the difficulty walking once he had "slept it off." The doctor paid no attention when I told him that Walter hadn't been drinking, that he wasn't under the influence of drugs, and that these problems had started just after the fight. The doctor sent us on our way with a few pills to ease the pain.

On the way home Walter's speech got worse and he started vomiting. He didn't want his wife to see him like this so I took him to the house of a go-go dancer who worked at the club and I had been seeing on the side. I put him to bed on the couch and went home to Nita, my wife. About two hours later I was awakened by a telephone call from the dancer telling me that Walter was dead. He had fallen asleep just after I left but he didn't seem right, so she tried to wake him up, but couldn't. She'd called the police but wanted me to come over immediately because she didn't like having a dead man in the house. I drove over, quieted her, and sent her back to her bedroom. Walter was lying on a long, green couch and appeared to be comfortably asleep. I felt his cold neck for a pulse and then sat down on the couch next to him and put his head in my lap. I put my arms around his shoulders and apologized for not jumping out of the car sooner and for not getting to him faster and for not insisting the doctor pay attention to us. We sat together like that for a long time while we waited for the police. Then I promised that nothing like this would ever happen to me again, that the world was going to change.

2

The Suicide Attempt

I seem to be floating, moving upward at an incredible rate. I break through some boundary and suddenly feel pain all around me, all through me and I cannot move or talk. I fight to clear my eyes but I can see only white and vague shapes and I hear nervous voices telling the anesthesiologist to give me more. I try to turn my head to find Harpo or Leonard Makowka, the surgeon, or my son or my wife, but can recognize no one. I feel about to explode then suddenly it's all over and I slowly start to descend.

"What the hell is this? Where the hell am I? Who the fuck are you? . . . Oh, *shit*, this thing hurts. Call that fat nurse back in here and tell her I'm dying. They stick me in this fucking room miles from the nurses' station. I'm fucking dying and they don't care, man. Who'd hear me if I had a stroke or a seizure or jumped out the window?"

"You've been calling the nurses every five minutes for the last twenty-four hours. They've had it. You've made two of them cry and one said she's calling in sick every day until you're out of here," he said.

"I've got a fucking hole in my belly and I'm in pain, OK? I don't want to be the most popular patient in the psych ward, I just want to feel no pain. If I'm so fucking obnoxious why don't they just knock me out?

"They're afraid that if they give you any more narcotics you'll stop breathing. Anyway, they're trying to detox you before you go to the recovery unit," he said.

"What? I'm not going to any recovery unit. I'm here because I had an accident with a knife. . . . I'm on methadone, man, I'm almost done with the program. I'm almost clean, I don't need this fucking psych hospital. I've got people waiting for me. I'm putting a new band together. When is my seventy-two-hour hold up? How long have I been here?"

"You're not on a seventy-two-hour hold," he said. "This isn't a psych hospital. You came in yesterday and had surgery in the afternoon."

"If I'm not on a seventy-two-hour hold then why the fuck am I tied down! Get me the fucking head nurse. Get me the fucking hospital administrator. Get me my lawyer."

"You've been out of it and tearing at your bandages. Your doctors ordered the restraints," he said.

"This is fucking incredible. My guts are on fire, the nurses are refusing to come in my room, I can't move, I'm tied down to the bed—this is kidnapping. You're going to prison, buddy. Not only are you going to rot in a fucking prison cell for the next twenty-five years, but I'm going to take you for everything you got, motherfucker, unless you let me out of these, right now!"

"Look, I can't do it. I'm just an aide here. I've got no say in the matter. The doctor will be by in an hour or so. Tell him."

"Yeah, right. That fucking sleazeball has to make a mortgage payment on the vacation home . . . he'll be real interested in getting me out of here fast. Man, I'm appealing to you as a human being. Look at me! Have you ever seen anything as miserable?" I felt completely trapped and the pain was making me panic. "Man, you wouldn't treat a dog this way. You can do something, I know you can. Something. *Anything.* Just give me something to tide me over until the nurse comes with the pain meds. Anything. I've got lots of money. My old lady will be by any minute with my money. Man, I'm in pain. Please?"

"I can't, I'm sorry, this is all I can do," he said, taking hold of my hand and looking at me sympathetically.

"Wow. That really helps. How's it feel? I can't feel it myself. Those damn ties cut off the circulation, the nerves are dead. Might as well just hack them off and give me a couple of hooks. Do they make hooks that can hold drumsticks?" Then an awful thought occurred to me. "You're not going to suggest that we pray or anything like that, are you?" I don't trust Christians. They're all repressed rapists — give them a cause and a crowbar and they crack skulls in the name of Jesus. "Well, I ain't going to God in this lifetime and for sure not in the next, so if you're planning on some Christian half nelson, get your ass straight out of here."

"I'm not a Christian," he said.

"I meant it generically. Moslem, Hindu, Baha'i — every religion known to man."

"I'm not religious," he said smiling.

"I'm lying here holding hands with a fucking heathen?" Now I realize what's going on. "Oh, no, don't tell me. Shit, I should have guessed . . . you're recovering."

"Five years, three months, and two weeks. Heroin. Just like you," he said, beaming.

31

"I haven't used heroin in a decade. This methadone program cured me of that shit. Hey! Look at the time! I'm due for my next dose."

"It's still about two hours away. How long have you been on methadone?" he asked.

"None of your business. Two *hours?* Why the fuck don't they have TVs in these rooms?" You fade from the public eye for even a minute and you're forgotten. "I'd have a fucking TV if I had my face on the cover of the *National Enquirer.*" I really can't take this anymore. "Look, man, do me a favor? Kill me. Just take that pillow and put it over my face and sit on it for half an hour. Make absolutely sure I'm dead before you remove it. I don't need any more brain damage." If I lose anymore brain cells I may no longer qualify as a member of the species.

"Did you try to kill yourself?" he asked.

"A vicious rumor. I was trying to open a bottle with a knife. It slipped. I'm here."

"I heard that you had a fight with your wife and then stabbed yourself."

"Sounds like that stupid bitch has been flapping her gums too much. If this is what you heard then how come I'm not on a seventy-two-hour hold in some psych hospital?"

"You will be if you try to sign out," he said.

"Ah! The fog lifts." Treachery . . . the lovely little wife. "Perhaps you should take some photographs of me urinating on myself or biting through my tongue in the throes of a grand mal seizure so she'll have a few fond reminders of this experience."

"Maybe she thinks you need help."

"She didn't seem to think that the other night when she slept while I bled. I was lying on the floor bleeding all night. Jesus! I woke up the next morning because a fucking cat stepped on the wound. Sounds like she cares a lot for my health. No, this is revenge, not concern. And you know what? You're no better. Look at you. Well, my life ain't some fucking movie-of-the-week about the rise and fall of a rock musician. So take that fucking smile off your face, and go on back to your books about Joplin and Hendrix and whoever the fuck else you think is cool, because they over- did it."

"Did you know them?" he asked.

"We all played canasta every Thursday night. Of course I fucking knew them." He's looking at me expectantly and I start doing a little quick thinking. "Look, I've got never- before-released tapes of Hendrix at my house. Untie these things and we'll go and listen to them. No one will know you did it. Shit, I've escaped from a dozen places just like this. Anyway, I've tried all these programs in the past. They never work and they cost a fucking fortune. . . . But, look, I swear, I'll come back when I'm ready. Honest. They'll take these off me tomorrow anyway, and I'll just get up and walk out then. The only difference between now and then is twenty-four hours and another grand that I don't have. Shit, I'll have to go score something and sell it to pay the fucking bill, so in a way you're turning me into a fucking dealer. Come on. We're wasting our time. You should hear Hendrix wail on this tape, man. On one of these songs he's got Janis and Cass singing backup."

I was only half-lying. I really did have Hendrix tapes at my house from a jam session we'd had in 1969 at Shady Oak, Stephen Stills's house in Studio City. Although it didn't include the all-star line-up of background vocals by other dead rock stars, it did include Buddy Miles and Rick James.

It was quite a night. I remember sitting there, taking a long hit off of one of Crosby's killer joints, vaguely aware that an argument was going on around me. "Fuck you!" "No, fuck *you*." "No, fuck you!" "That's a cop out, man!" said Stephen, getting the last word.

"What the fuck are these guys talking about?" I wondered, vaguely. Man, this shit is so strong, it's almost too strong. Then the thought hit me—I can't talk, I've forgotten how to talk. I need help. "Somebody help me!" I silently begged, trying to make my jaw work.

"Come on D, let's get the fuck out of here and play some music," said Stephen.

"Sure man, let's go," I said. Thank God, I can talk! "Where are we going?"

"Hendrix is here," Stephen said. "He's been waiting in the music room for an hour."

The music room at Stephen's smelled like a mixture of locker room, incense, pot, and booze. We'd nailed old persian rugs to the walls to muffle the noise and the room was forever dank and muggy. As we walked in, I saw Hendrix sitting on one of Stephen's amps, playing his ass off, while Buddy Miles was literally pounding the shit out of my drums. It was very loud and hurt my ears. I didn't think that Hendrix liked me very much, because of Denise. In general, he struck me as an extremely unhappy person, kind of scared. He always had a guitar in his hands—unless he was getting high or getting laid.

Jimi stopped playing when we walked into the room. There was a big pile of cocaine on a mirror sitting on top of the B3 organ and we all gathered around and took turns snorting from it. "So, you guys gigging yet?" Jimi asked Stephen. *Snort.*

"Nah, we're still working shit out. We can't find a bass player," Stephen said. *Sniff.*

"Yeah," said Jimi, "that's the story of my life. There's a definite shortage of bass players." *Snort.*

"Rick James is a great bass player," said Stephen to Jimi as he glanced toward Rick, "but he's doing his own thing. And besides, Rick says he has a kid from Detroit named Greg Reeves that he wants us to check out. . . . Hey! Where's the Jack Daniels? Bruce — get us some more J.D.!!

We played off and on that night. Mostly we attended to the coke on the B3. But I do have tapes.

"CSN is one of my favorite all-time bands. You guys were my teenage years. *Deja Vu* is without question my favorite all-time album. Time has sure changed them, though. Tell me something. How fat can Stephen Stills get?"

"What?"

"The guy gets fatter by the second. Every time you see him in *Rolling Stone* or in a video you think, 'This is it. He can't get any fatter without blowing up,' and then you see him a month later and he's put on another hundred pounds. I mean, it's depressing to see him and Crosby. They remind an entire generation that we're all slowly dying. They ought to be considerate enough to grow old gracefully or keep out of sight," he said.

"Man, this is not going to work. You can't distract me, no way you can out-manipulate me. You let me out of these things now, or I'll tell your boss, your wife, and everyone you know that you pulled down my pants and went down on me while I was strapped down. I'll fucking press charges and you'll never work in a place like this again."

"People should grow old with dignity. Have you seen those three guys lately? They look like the Three Stooges. You half expect them to start hitting each other with hammers and tire irons."

While Stephen was in control, there wasn't any arguing in the band and they were still into complimenting each other. Stephen called Graham "razor throat" for his uncanny ability to hit the high notes and cut through the music. Stephen was clearly recognized as the best songwriter by David and Graham; it was a real mutual admiration society for a while. But then things started getting out of hand, and the arguments among them got stuck in the "fuck you", "no, fuck *you*" groove. Very unproductive. Stephen was losing control and at times, acting a bit strange.

"I used to be in the CIA," said Stephen to the cute blonde that had followed us home. She was one of the types we used to call "coke whores," because they'd do anything to be around rock stars and cocaine. "Yeah," Stephen continued, "Special Forces, Vietnam. I'm a colonel." At first when he went on like that it was funny, and I'd really get a kick out of watching the girl's eyes widen as she'd say, "*Wow!* How cool!" But Stephen kept telling people that story and then I started getting worried when he began pulling out a uniform to show them. I began getting a sinking feeling that things were about to go haywire and I knew that if Stephen lost control of the band it wouldn't be long before the managers moved in to take over—and then God knows what else.

Another thing that at first seemed like a joke but which got a bit out of hand, was our conversations in Spanish. When we'd be drunk and really high on coke Stephen, who'd lived in Central America, would start speaking Spanish to me. Since I'm half Spanish, he just assumed I understood, but I didn't know a word of the language, so usually I'd just say "si." But sometimes I'd find myself trying to carry on my end of the conversation, mumbling in some strange dialect of Spanishlike sounds and Stephen would answer me back. "Jesus," I'd think, "we really are too high."

"What happened to you? Why'd you leave them?" he asked.

I don't want to think about this stuff any more. "Fuck you! I am dead serious—let me out *now*."

"I'm your one-on-one while you're here. The doctor and your wife think you're a danger to yourself, and I know you are. I was a junkie for ten years, and I have already said or heard everything you have said or will say, so nothing in this fucking world can make me remove those restraints. Now, we've got two hours to kill before you can get any pain meds, and the best way to kill them is to talk, so start answering my questions or I'm going to get a Bible and start reading the whole fucking thing to you. Why did you leave CSN&Y when they were the biggest band in the world?" he asked.

"Did you know that your right eye closes all the way when you're angry?" He looks like someone taking aim. I need time to think. "I'll bet you've killed somebody. I came close once, but I was too fucked up to load the gun in time. Couldn't find the bullets. He was five miles away before I got the thing cocked. Anyway, I left the group because Neil thought Stephen was fucking his wife. And Neil got pissed off." Neil was definitely the jealous type, a broody, intense personality. He'd joined up with us while we were working in Sag Harbor, and when we first moved the CSN operation out to the West Coast I stayed at Neil's house in Topanga Canyon. It was OK until his wife got a bit flirty with me, which did *not* please Neil. Life there became very uncomfortable, so I left. By that time Stephen had rented Shady Oak from Peter Tork of the Monkees. Peter had bought the house from Wally Cox, for whom it was built. It was the biggest, most beautiful house I had ever lived in.

"So what?" he said.

"So, Neil was pissed off. This sort of thing often pisses off husbands. When Stephen knocked up my wife it pissed me off for well over a week." Actually, she wasn't my wife at that time, but I was madly in love with Laura. She and her identical twin sister, Lorna, were practically part of the furnishings at Stephen's house. They both fucked the entire band, and when Laura got pregnant we didn't know whose it was. But when the baby was born, a beautiful girl we named Jennifer, she looked just like Stephen and I was really pissed at him for that. My sister, Darlene, took Jennifer and raised her, and I stayed with Laura. One morning, she shook me awake and gave me the ultimatum—"marry me or else." So, with enough downs in my system to ease a terrific hangover, I found myself in front of a preacher for a second time.

"Anyway, Neil got angry and wanted Stephen dead, or at least out of the group and someone clever in management suggested that a compromise might be better than dismantling this money-making machine and someone else suggested that the perfect compromise would be to kick Stephen's favorite drummer out of the group and everyone thought that fair and equitable and I was out." Yeah, and next to the death of my mother, this had to be the most horrible incident of my entire life.

It happened sometime in the middle of winter on a cold, but really beautiful day. I had just traded in my Porsche for a 1964 Ferrari GTB-4—just like one Stephen had had—and I drove it up to the CSN&Y office on LaCienga for what promised to be a heavy duty meeting. A few days earlier we had gotten back from a tour that had ended abruptly in Denver when Neil walked off the stage swearing he'd never work with Stephen again. CSN&Y had fallen apart. Stephen and I flew back to L.A. together, and he had cried the whole way. "Don't worry, man," I told him. "Fuck 'em! We'll start a new band, a kick-ass rock & roll band with no wimpy harmonies. We don't need them, we're stars. We'll get anyone we want."

But somehow, as I was pulling up in my car, I got the feeling that something was about to go terribly wrong. I walked up the stairs and through the door and the first thing I saw was a pile of gold albums still in their brown wrapping paper, lined up against the wall. They were for *Deja Vu* and I knew one of them had my name on it. As I entered the room the girl at the desk gave me a funny look and I saw that the door to Elliot Roberts' office was closed. "What's up?" I asked.

"They're all in there," she said. "Stephen, Graham, David, Neil, and Geffen. The door's locked and you can't go in."

"The fuck I can't," I yelled, reaching for the door. Just then it opened and they all filed out. Not one of them would look at me.

Then Stephen said, "The fat guys with the cigars said if we don't finish the tour, we'll all go back to being broke hippies. Dallas . . . D, Neil said if he has to work with me, you have to go. . . ." His voice trailed off.

"What do you mean 'go'?" I said, fighting tears.

"You're fired," Stephen said, almost in a whisper. "I'm sorry, man, I really am, but we had no choice."

I stood there, open-mouthed and uncomprehending. A wave of nausea came over me and I felt ridiculous and stupid.

Suddenly I realized with a shock something I had always known in my gut—that band was my whole world and that world had just crashed to an end. Then I thought it must be a horrible mistake; they'll realize they really need me, they'll beg me to come back. But that only worked for a minute and then I thought, "Oh, *Jesus*, what *now!*" and a terrible loneliness joined the nausea.

I walked down the stairs and got in my Ferrari and went to find something to ease the pain.

"Y'know they say sex and drugs and rock & roll cause trouble, but it's only the sex part that can really get you into trouble. There's no way of predicting the consequences of putting your dick where it doesn't belong. There's no such thing as free love—or free lust. There's always a price."

"What was your price?" the man beside me asked.

"Open your eyes, man. Look at me. I've got no money, no friends, probably no wife, no chance of convincing anyone in the music business that I'm worth taking a risk on. I'm strapped down to a bed in some shit-ass hospital because I tried to off myself and all I can think about is getting high. The express train to hell."

"What? You're blaming all this on *promiscuity?*" he asked.

"I blame it on, I blame it on . . . the sixties." Yeah—the sixties. Why take any personal blame when you can pass it off on a decade? "Yeah, it's the fucking sixties! I was young and stupid and I swallowed the whole 'dawn of a new day, it's a new world' bullshit hook, line, and sinker. I *believed*. People were good . . . no one would intentionally harm anyone else . . . we would discover the way through our poets and prophets. Man, I was just like someone who enlisted in the army because they thought it was the right thing to do. I went in naive and trusting and came out betrayed, bitter, and barely alive." Wow. I *liked* this analogy. "They got gold medals for putting their lives on the line. Well, I got seven gold and two platinum records. And don't think going up in front of an audience isn't putting your life on the line – there's nothing scarier. Why the hell do you think Crosby keeps getting arrested for carrying guns? It's not all drug-induced para-noia. Look at Lennon. Remember Altamont? We were there. Charles Manson supposedly had a hit list that we were on. We all carried guns, man. The war machine wanted us shut up because we were making noise to stop their war and the nuts out there wanted to get their faces on the cover of *Time* magazine. We were walking targets." I *really* like this analogy. "I've got a 'delayed stress reaction' or what else do they call it? 'Post-traumatic stress disorder.' I am a POW – a Prisoner of Woodstock. There are thousands of us out there. We should organize, get government funding, have parades."

"Why'd you try to off yourself?" he asked.

He is fishing for compliments. I'll give him what he wants. "Nothing gets by you, does it? OK, I'll tell you, if you promise not to tell anyone and if after I'm done you'll go get the nurse because something major is happening in my gut and I am going to need a ponderosa-sized bedpan any second. All right? Deal? Good.

"I don't really know why I tried this time, I've tried lots of times. Overdoses mostly, ten, maybe twenty times. Well, I guess I do know. . . ." He's going to love this. "This time I think it was because I had one of those lucid moments that I always try to avoid. You know, when the fog clears and you're able to see how things really are and what you've become?

41

"I was drinking with a drinking buddy and we were really fucking drunk. I was also doing cocaine. We went down to the corner liquor store to get some more vodka but when we got there we discovered we were out of money. I went in and stood by the check-out line, put out my hand, and started begging for money. No big deal, I've probably done it before, but all of a sudden—*wham!*—I'm having an out-of-body experience and I'm watching myself beg! When no one comes across with the money. I get mad and start telling people who I am and what I want . . . like they owe me!

" 'I'm Dallas Taylor! Gimme twenty dollars!' Not only am I pitiful because of the begging, but I also see myself as a pathetic, whining baby that still believes the world owes him something. Then, in stumbles my friend and I see myself in twenty years. I walk out of the place, throw my keys and wallet as far as I can, stagger home, which is only a few blocks, smash in the front door, go to the kitchen for a butcher's knife, and shove it in my gut. I laid down on the floor and waited to die. When I woke up the next morning the desire to be dead was not as strong as the pain in my belly and I called for someone and came here. End of story.

"Oh, oh. You'd better get the nurse, something big is about to blow. Look, I told you my story. I won't leave. I'll probably leave with everyone's permission tomorrow."

By the time he'd stepped into the hall I'd wriggled out of the restraints. Before he'd taken five steps toward the nurses' station, I was out the first floor window, my butt hanging out of the hospital gown, my jeans and sneakers tucked under my arm, leaving a small trail of blood behind from the IV I'd just pulled out of my yellow hand.

3

Safety in Numbers

Again I feel myself surfacing, breaking through this anesthesia pool, trying to remember where I am. The sounds of the surgeons' voices remind me and I want to ask them how it's going, but I can't move or speak. I remember my resolve that I would not review my life, but something stronger has taken hold. I've been swimming in an audio-visual extravaganza. The possibility that it is, in fact, death that is accessing my memory banks is, of course, very real and frightening. All I can do is trust that the survival instinct that has pulled me through so many deadly situations is at the controls. I watch the images and wait for clues. My sister, Darlene, drifts by waving, and I follow her as she swims deeper into the waters.

My sister has told me that I used to fake stomachaches to get paregoric. When my mother finally figured out what I was doing, she was worried that I'd turn out like both of her brothers who were only in their thirties when they died of alcoholism. They died in our house on Drexel Avenue in San

Antonio within a year of each other, when I was seven, and then eight. I remember my grandmother, Mercedes Cantu, a dark and impressive Spanish woman, blaming the death of her sons on "evil alcohol" and making me promise that I would never drink. The first time that I broke that promise to her was right after my mother's death. I was living in Arizona with my father, and one day, instead of going to school, I went to a liquor store with a kid named Rick and stole a large bottle of malt liquor. I downed the whole thing and though I hated the taste, I liked the sense of well-being that came so quickly. So I went and got more and did it again and passed out.

I repeated this ritual nearly every weekend until I got my first taste of marijuana. I got it from an older friend named Billy who played the bass guitar and was one of the coolest of the "too cool for school" group. He carried it around in Prince Albert Tobacco cans. One day he gave me a hit and then one afternoon he gave me a joint and an important relationship was begun. I loved marijuana. I had never felt so comfortable, so at ease, so content. I loved everything about it: the soothing effect, the thrill of the possibility of getting caught, the forgetfulness. I smoked pot constantly, and I sampled everything else that Billy pushed in my face: uppers, downers, prescription drugs, over-the-counter cold medicines. Finally, I experienced my first hallucination when Billy scored some form of medication or pesticide that supposedly had belladonna in it. We paid no attention to the warning on the side — "Not to be ingested" — or the skull and crossbones just above it, and swallowed two tablespoonsful apiece. Soon, strange looking, argumentative people appeared from thin air and began conversations that made no sense but were highly entertaining. These new friends became frequent visitors, and then the jump to LSD was only natural. Soon acid and marijuana were daily companions, and I would stay high for weeks at a time, forgetting or avoiding everything else including school, friends, eating, and girls. My next true romance didn't occur until just after I'd turned twenty, when a friend introduced me to a lovely lady named cocaine and we became inseparable.

When I awoke, John's tent was even more humid and the Indian print pillows were wet with my sweat. The air was thick and heavy with the odors of hash and the teeming crowd, and my head pounded with what felt like jet lag but was actually a combination of anxiety, exhaustion, and reality. I could hear in the distance a stage announcement cautioning everyone against consuming a bad acid that was in circulation. John and the others had left. I was embarrassed that I had allowed exhaustion to get the better of me and hurt that the party had moved on without me, and decided I needed a quick cure for what ailed me. My rule was, When in doubt, always choose cocaine and always do one line more than you think you should, because it's never quite enough. I headed for the tent flap and was almost out when my foot was grabbed by someone half covered with pillows. I looked down and saw the teenage girl Graham had been ogling before she passed out.

"You're the drummer," she said groggily.

"That's right," I answered, as I freed my foot and moved to go on my way.

"Wait!" she said. "I like drummers. They got big arms and they're stupid." She attempted to struggle to her feet but passed out halfway up and fell with a thud on the cushions. I stepped over her and had almost made it outside when another female face appeared at the tent flap.

"She's right," the face said, "Don't hold it against her for telling it straight. This world needs more truth."

"And more kindness," I said. As I pushed past her, she grabbed my arm. She was short and fair skinned with braided blond hair crowned by a leather head band with white peace symbols on it. She was older for a groupie, maybe twenty-five, with a gap between her front teeth and the gaunt yellow frailty of a junkie.

"I'll show you some kindness, baby," she said, putting her hands on my waist. "I haven't had a drummer since Keith Moon."

"Well, I hear Keith is here, so why not hit him up for a repeat performance?" I said.

"Not enough time. Too many people to experience. Your name is Dallas, right? Before Crosby, Stills, Nash and Young, you were with . . . Clear Water," she said, fishing for something in her purse.

"Clear Light," I corrected her.

"Right. A minor band. You were good, though. I saw you in New York. Here it is! See! You're on my list!" My name was number twenty-two on a list of thirty names. Number one was Janis Joplin.

"So what, you want my autograph?" I asked. She started laughing and then coughing and finally gagging.

"I was hoping for something a little more personal to remember you by," she said, swallowing hard and trying to strike a seductive pose. She had no idea what she looked like — like she needed a week of sleep, a month of good meals, and a transfusion or two.

"I'll send you a photograph," I said as I left the tent. The crowds winding through the tents seemed less attractive and expectant than a few hours before. The day seemed old and tired and the heat and dirt made everyone appear less hopeful as they trudged along in slow motion. I definitely needed the magic brought back to this scene; I needed the shimmer and transforming wizardry of cocaine. I needed my medicine. I turned around and reentered the tent.

In the ten seconds since I'd left the woman had tied off her right arm and was about to put a needle in a fat vein in her hand. I watched her silently as she punctured the yellow skin, drew blood into the syringe already filled with a clear fluid, and then in a slow, loving gesture, gently pushed it all into her bloodstream. There was something very sexual about the act itself as well as her reaction as the effect took hold. She closed her eyes, arched her head back, and rocked slightly, back and forth . . . back and forth. She hugged herself and turned in a circle and appeared to be dancing to an internal music. She seemed absolutely alone and content and no longer appeared frail and sickly. She pivoted and opened her eyes; seeing me, she held wide her arms to welcome me in her dance. I took her in my arms and slowly turned with her while untying her arm and placing pressure on her bleeding hand.

"Come with me," she whispered in my ear. "It's beautiful." I'd never used a needle before. I knew it was a hang-up, that I'd probably soon get over it, but I wasn't ready for it now.

"Take me half way there," I said. "Give me cocaine." She opened her eyes and smiled. She was now completely in command and she laughed and held me firm in her grip for several more turns before she stopped and retrieved from her purse a brown glass vial filled with white powder. She handed me a small knife to scoop it out with, which I did several times, and in a very few seconds the brightness and clarity returned to the world and I felt ready to take on just about anything.

"What's your name?" I asked her as she started unbuttoning her blouse.

"Guinnevere," she said. "Where do you want me?"

"In your clothes and outside with me looking for something to eat," I said. The cocaine would soon take away my appetite. I hadn't eaten for a day or two and my body needed some nourishment before I went on stage or it wouldn't work right. The heroin had brought Guinnevere either tolerance of or indifference to my rejection of her and she serenely acquiesced. We held hands as we exited and she sang David's "Guinnevere" as we walked through the crowd.

We stopped very near the stage at a small green tent that was filled with people Guinnevere knew, and we ate plates of roasted vegetables and cheese. Bruce Berry, a new roadie of ours who couldn't have been more than eighteen years old, appeared from nowhere and sat down next to me. He was the younger brother of Jan Berry of Jan and Dean, a bright, golden sort of kid from a wealthy Bel Air family who just wanted to follow music for the rest of his life. Bruce and I had struck up a quick and easy friendship.

"Hey, man, where's the party?" he asked, sitting down. His eyes were red and barely open. Clearly, he had been having more fun than I had.

"Right here, man," I said. "Look around you. This is the way the world is going to be for the rest of your fucking life."

"Far out," he said, and reached over and grabbed a handful of food off my plate and put it into his mouth.

"Hey! There's nothing but vegetables in my mouth!" he said, a look of disgust on his face. Unlike most of the people we traveled with, Bruce and I were devoted carnivores, and meat was part of each meal. I handed him the bottle of Chianti that was being circulated and told him to swallow them, like a pill, and then I turned my attention back to Guinnevere. I took her hand again and while she was involved in a conversation with a woman who closely resembled her, I examined it. I was amazed how small and fine the bones were. She had expensive rings on each finger which were too big and which, I thought, were probably meant to draw eyes away from her bruised and swollen veins. She also wore too many leather and macrame bracelets and looking under them I found several scars from deep knife wounds on her wrist. She turned her hand slightly to obscure my view and then pulled me over to meet a conservatively dressed woman, who was roughly her age.

"Dallas, this is Marilyn. We went to school together." Marilyn indifferently put out her hand. She was slightly overweight with short, dark hair and glasses, and she resembled a librarian. Marilyn was the only woman with a bra on for fifteen miles and everything she wore seemed to be exactly one size too small. Consequently, her body gave the impression of trying to break free.

"Pretty heavy scene," she said uncomfortably, trying to appear friendly. She obviously didn't like being here or talking to me, and the jargon was awkward.

"Dallas is the drummer for a new group that's going to be playing later and Marilyn was my roommate at Smith until I dropped out. Have you seen Abby?" Guinnevere said, as she pulled free her hand and headed off in another direction.

"Abby is her daughter," said Marilyn disapprovingly.

"Never in the history of man have there ever been this many people in one place without a riot starting," said a shirtless, bearded, blond man sitting in the lotus position, eating a handful of raw, unwashed green beans.

"I can't believe she went to Smith," I said.

"Her name was Sheila then and she was an economics major. Real potential. She started doing drugs, and now. . . ."

"Ever tried them yourself?" I asked. "They might set you free."

"I'm not feeling the least bit oppressed, thank you," she said. Clearly she resented my question and just as clearly she resented me for being a long hair, a male, and a Southerner. There was also something almost uncomfortably familiar about her, and then I realized that she reminded me of Laura Nyro, who wouldn't talk to me anymore.

I had actually met Laura Nyro through David Geffen, and I was involved with her for about six months. She lived just off Central Park in New York City, in an apartment near Judy Collins, and Stephen and I often took the same limousine to visit them. At first glance you would see Laura as a plain woman. She was overweight and had a large nose but she had dark silky hair down to her ass, exquisitely feminine hands and was quite sexy in the way she carried herself. She was a strong woman, too, and I loved her voice. She didn't mind that I was recently separated from my wife and two kids and was living with another woman. She didn't mind my lack of education or my youth. She did mind that I was doing drugs and when I mentioned to her one night on the phone that I'd just bought my first ounce of cocaine, she said she never wanted to see me again and hung up. I hadn't talked to her since, and so the opportunity of convincing this Nyro surrogate that drugs were the answer, not the problem, was appealing.

"What's the name of your band?" she asked.

"Crosby, Stills, and Nash and Young," I said.

"Never heard of you." she said. "I like California music. Mamas and Papas, Beach Boys, Jan and Dean, John Sebastian, the Beatles. There's a group!" she said.

"They did all of *Sgt. Pepper's* on drugs," I said. "Without drugs they'd still be singing about wanting to hold your hand."

"I don't believe you," she said, turning away. She was looking at her watch. She was every bit as intransigent as Laura, and my grandmother.

"I know John Sebastian. He's a good friend of mine," I said. "He actually discovered me." She turned toward me and seemed interested for the first time.

"I just left his tent. I'll take you back to meet him," I said. She almost smiled and I felt forgiveness and acceptance right around the corner, and then Guinnevere returned with her daughter. Abby looked about four years old. She was blonde and naked and dirty. Guinnevere was stumbling and smiling broadly, her eyes almost completely shut. We all watched as the two of them danced together in the mud.

"Far out," said Bruce.

"Man, that's beautiful," I echoed.

"Revolting," said Marilyn. "She ought to have that poor child taken away from her."

Intent on the rhythm and clearly not comprehending her degree of impairment, Guinnevere whirled until she stumbled into a small cooking stove and cut her shin. While people were running about trying to come up with the best way to stop the bleeding, she started vomiting, and Abby started crying. When Marilyn saw Guinnevere was hurt, she tore a strip off her shirt and applied it to the wound. The bleeding stopped but the vomiting continued and this, coupled with Guinnevere's confusion and a fresh needle mark on her left arm, convinced me that she'd overdosed.

"We'd better get her to one of the medical tents," I said.

"It's just a small wound. It doesn't need any stitches," Marilyn said.

"She's overdosed," I said.

"You can't do that on marijuana," she said.

"You can on heroin," I said.

"Heroin?"

"Heroin!" I pointed out the fresh needle mark. She slapped Guinnevere across the face.

"You stupid bitch!" she screamed, as she slapped her again. Bruce pulled her away.

"It happens," he said, trying to hold her arms.

"You stay with the kid, we'll take her to a first aid station," I said.

"Heroin! You're a junkie! A lousy junkie!" she shrieked, fighting Bruce.

"Hey, it's no big deal! It happens to the best of us," he said.

I lifted Guinnevere easily. I could feel the bones in her back and her ribs through her clothing. She was awake enough to put her arms around my neck and hum softly in my ear. We headed toward the very rear of the stage where I thought I remembered seeing a Red Cross sign.

"Wait! We're coming with you!" Marilyn shouted. She had Abby in her arms and was dragging Bruce, who was still trying to hold onto her. Santana was playing and the crowd behind the stage was thick and difficult to get through. By the time we found the tent, Guinnevere was asleep and her breathing was shallow. I put her on a cot and a nurse took her pulse and blood pressure. She got from Marilyn and me what medical history she could, then hooked Guinnevere up to an IV and gave her a series of injections. A hippie doctor came over and gave her yet another injection and smiled at us as he moved on to another overdose.

"She'll be all right," he said. "Come back in an hour and she'll be sitting up and talking." Still eager to win Marilyn over, I suggested we continue our walk toward John's tent, but she wanted none of it.

"I've seen enough of this," she said. "This is all very sick and sad and I just want to wait here until she's well enough to leave."

"And then what?" I asked.

"And then . . . I'm going to take her home and get her help. Professional help." She sat down, with the squirming Abby on her lap.

"She's a junkie," Bruce said. "She doesn't want help. She either wants to see God or she wants to die."

"Get out of here!" she yelled. "You're both so matter-of-fact about this it makes me sick!"

"No judgments, man," said Bruce. "It ain't good or bad. It just is."

"You're wrong. It's wrong. Look at this," she said, pointing to Abby. "All of this is very bad. All of this is wrong."

"What a downer," said Bruce. "Let's get out of here, man. She's a real bummer." Bruce started to leave and I followed him out but I began wondering who was right. Certainly my parents weren't right. Then I thought of my own kids, Dallas, Jr., and Sharlotte, and wondered how they'd turn out. Nita was still attractive and she would easily find another man to take care of her. She was a good woman and a good mother and the kids were probably better off away from me. My side of the family was depressed and bitter alcoholics who all died long before they had the luxury of a midlife crisis. I reasoned that if this same emotional time bomb that I was certain was inside me were a product of environment rather than genetics, then perhaps the distance from me would protect them. Also, the kids produced in me a suffocating sense of responsibility that was not at all consistent with my image of the private life of a rock star. I needed to be free to pursue every kind of sexual and emotional experience available to me. It was not only my right, it was my responsibility to my creativity and to my generation. Besides, I was now in love with Laura, who with her twin sister, Lorna, was living with me at Stephen's house in Los Angeles.

Laura and Lorna were sixteen and drop-dead gorgeous, real Hollywood kids, with long dark hair and green eyes and perfect bodies. They were willing to partake in any party, drug, or sex act we could come up with. They loved to snort cocaine and fuck and if you were lucky, you could do it with both of them at the same time. Their favorite game was swapping boyfriends and seeing how long it took you to figure out which girl was which. When Stephen and I would pull into the driveway in his big Mercedes 600 Limo after a night, or sometimes a day and night, at Wally Heider's recording studio, Laura and Lorna would run down to meet us—butt naked. We'd strip down and swim in the pool and have breakfast and it was perfect. I was only twenty-one, but I'd been supporting myself for six years, married for five, and a father for four, and Laura's wildness made me feel like a teenager again. This made her as invaluable to my new lifestyle and image as my new Ferrari. My kids would survive and, in fact, probably thrive. I put them out of my mind and followed Bruce to the security check behind the stage. The guilt that I felt had nothing to do with this new day and had to be ignored. Besides, guilt had already taken me places I never wanted to be.

It was guilt that had gotten me married to Nita and stuck with two kids in the first place. On the day I got married the only person who had anything to celebrate was my sister Darlene. With my mother dead and my father grieving the mistake he saw I was about to make, only Darlene had the energy and the interest to organize a ceremony and a reception. She found a Baptist minister who wasn't bothered by marrying a sixteen-year-old boy to a pregnant fifteen-year-old girl and she invited everyone she could think of to the church on that warm spring day. My father arrived looking beaten and disappointed, and he sat between his disinterested wife and the bubbling Darlene who was decked out in a hat that resembled a pillow with a veil. I arrived a half hour late and very stoned and right away I noticed that Nita's side of the church was empty. Her father had given her fifty dollars for a dress to be married in, but he refused to be shamed by publicly sanctioning this flushing away of his daughter's life. Nita was a pretty girl with hazel eyes and dark hair. We had met three months earlier on a date that Darlene had arranged, and we were standing in front of the preacher solely due to my persuasiveness and raging hormones. There was no love, only obligation, and Nita knew it, which made me both sad and angry. Yet Nita, who lived for marriage and motherhood, had so little self-esteem that she actually thought she'd done well for herself.

The reception for about ten people was at my sister's house, and Darlene kept crying and kissing everyone every few minutes. I stayed stoned the entire day, feeling alternately grown-up and trapped, and determined not to let this change my life. I was getting out of all of this. I was not going to have the life of my mother or my father or my grandparents or Darlene or anyone that I knew. I was not going to live a small, sad life in a small, sad town, and then lay waiting for death with nothing to remember or forget.

After our three-day honeymoon in Scottsdale, I moved Nita into a small apartment and almost immediately went out on the road with my band. Darlene located me by phone in some tiny Arizona town about a month later and told me that Nita had miscarried. I was deeply relieved, but when Darlene put Nita on the phone, I told Nita not to worry, that it was not meant to be this time but that we would try again. I continued on the road for quite some time with little success but with many affairs and one-night stands. I returned to Phoenix to find Nita healthy, happy, and ready to take me at my word. She reassured me that babies were fun and wouldn't affect my playing, and convinced me that what was missing in my life was a family. Three months later she was pregnant again, and again having difficulty with bleeding and cramps. To save the pregnancy, the doctor ordered an indefinite period of bed rest, which afforded me the opportunity to play and whore around in Phoenix rather than in some backwater a hundred miles away.

It was during this time that my father was killed. I was coming back home after a wild night and most of a day with a dancer named Donna, driving in my Mustang, doing almost twice the speed limit, when the news bulletin interrupted the rock & roll on the radio. My father, who was a stunt pilot, had crashed that afternoon at an airshow at a military base in Tucson. They said he was there to represent the United States in an airshow competition with the Soviet Union, and then they mentioned his war record. They described the ball of flame that had engulfed the plane after it crashed into the field and said authorities speculated that the cause of the crash was mechanical failure, not pilot error. Finally, they mentioned his survivors, sending the station's condolences to me and Darlene and our stepmother. I felt sorry for his wife, who would have a very difficult time getting along without him, and felt sorry for Darlene who was reared by both him and my mother. I even felt a little sadness myself, although for many years there had been nothing but anger between my father and me.

At one time, all I wanted was to be just like him, a stunt pilot flying through the air. I'd fly in make-believe cockpits I made out of cardboard boxes, and when my father flew in to get me and take me for a visit, he'd sometimes let me take the controls. By the time I was working for my mother's boy-friend, Fricke, I had become less and less happy with my father, but I still wanted to fly. Fricke would often let me practice with his training flight simulator. When my mother died, my father flew out for the funeral. I had already told him that I didn't want to leave Texas, that I wanted to live with Darlene and keep playing in my band, and he had agreed. But after the funeral, he insisted that we go for a quick flight and while we were up in the air he told me that he had lied and that I was on my way to Arizona to live with him. Right there I lost all desire to fly and I lost my faith in the sky.

The announcement was over, the music was back on, and I found myself feeling really sad, because it made me think about Fricke, and how he had died in his crop duster years before. I wished that I felt as bad now as I had then. I also found myself wondering where my father's teeth had ended up. Then I turned the car around and headed back to Donna's.

I followed Bruce to the back of the stage, and when I saw he was getting hassled by some security types who were not going to let us up to watch, I called to Chip Monck. Chip, who was standing shirtless on stage reading announcements, was the stage manager, and he was also our tour manager, so he waved us past the knot of security people and pointed to an area where we could comfortably stand. I hesitated looking at the audience at first for fear of provoking the panic I always felt before performing, but Bruce's reaction convinced me to take a chance.

"Unbelievable, man," he said. "This is far-fucking-out. This must be hippie heaven." I slowly turned my gaze up from the ground and, peeking through partially closed eyelids, and I saw more flesh than I'd ever seen in my life. The faces stretched from a fence just in front of the large wooden stage to a ridge about a half mile straight ahead, then continued less densely beyond. It was a vast stretch of smiling heads and animated figures that appeared both uniform and unique. It was a vast picnic. There was nothing to fear here.

Chip Monck kept talking, giving the locations of tents with free food and drink, and urging people to share what they had. While he spoke, up and down the fat lines of people along the rim of the stage, pipes and cigarettes and bottles and cans were passed, not a single person taking more than what seemed his fair share. Far above us hovered a vast white tarpaulin strung between poles and towers, shading the stage, gently billowing in the warm wind, appearing like an enormous white bird. Something *was* happening here, and it was not hype, not business. There was magic in this summer air and one could become intoxicated by a single breath. I now understood John's childlike excitement and Stephen's need to focus on something so simple and unimportant as money. This army of people was overwhelming because they were us. They believed in what we believed in and they knew and

believed in our music and they were not a hundred aficionados gathered in a college gymnasium to hear Richie
Havens or Country Joe, or even twenty thousand straining
to hear the Who or Janis or Jimi in some arena. They were
a generation whose time had come and the "dawn of a
new day" made sense to me now. I belonged. Something very
good was going to happen and these people would take
me there.

4

The Awakening

I am floating through this moving-picture pool and I wonder if there's another problem with the anesthesia or if the operation is over. The liquid is thick and the swim arduous. I get close enough to the surface to hear voices and I am starting to feel pain but still I cannot see what is going on. The voices directed at me are soft and reassuring, and I feel myself being wheeled from the room. I guess this means that the operation is over and I struggle to move my head, my hands, my feet. They do not respond and I panic. I open my mouth to tell everyone that the operation has left me quadriplegic. I discover that it won't work either and I feel trapped. The pain is increasing and there is no solution other than diving back into my pool.

"I can't make it!" I said. "It's too hard. I'm in too much pain."

"You can do it," she said, putting the hospital slippers on my feet. "I'll help you. It will make you feel much better."

"I can't. I can't do it." I choked back a few fake sobs and coughed a little, simulating vomiting. That usually worked and then the staff would just leave me alone. But not this one. Instead of comforting me, she pinched me hard on the arm.

"Ow!" I cried angrily, turning to see what was going on. "What the fuck are you doing?"

"There! See how much more painful a silly little pinch was than what's going on in your belly? Upsy-daisy," she said too cheerfully as she pulled me to my feet. Her face was inches from mine and her breath smelled of too many un-filtered Camels and at least one bad tooth. She had probably been pretty about twenty years ago but her skin was now deeply lined and blotchy, her long bleached-blond hair thin and broken, and the pounds of makeup she'd inexpertly trowelled on made her look like a whore with cataracts. Her name was Candy and she'd been with a motorcycle gang shooting dope for fifteen years and was sober now for three. She still dressed like a tough and cheap teenage girl in too-tight jeans, a long-sleeved T-shirt and black cowboy boots. Minutes ago she had told me she would be my counselor while I was in the detox unit and if there was anything I needed I shouldn't hesitate to contact her. She then told me in the same sickeningly sweet voice that if I ever even thought of breaking any of the rules, she'd be all over me like "an ugly rash." She was either very clever or quite disturbed and I had no idea yet how to play her. I would have to go along for a while and see.

"These groups give you the opportunity to share your feelings with others and to gain some perspective on what a mess you've made of your life," she said.

"I've stayed fucked-up for twenty years precisely to avoid these things. I've gotten very good at it and I don't want to change this," I said, feeling very poetic and proud of myself both for standing up to her and for getting out what sounded like my first coherent sentence of the day. My head was thick with the smog generated by an unlubricated broken-down mind that was unaccustomed to working without drugs. Six cups of coffee and a pack of cigarettes had at least turned the thing on, but thoughts were painful, realizations clearly impossible, and more than anything it yearned to be shut down and ignored.

"That's why you're here," she said in that same sugary tone. "You're a runner. A wimp. A worm with no backbone who'd rather lie in a pile of shit than strain a little to see what's outside it."

"Say what?" I said. She smiled innocently as she tied my bathrobe belt.

"The truth is the truth no matter how it's said. Now you can leave your cigarettes here because smoking isn't allowed in the group room," she said ripping the pack from my hand and throwing it on the bed.

"Now wait one fucking minute!" Every joint in my body ached and every muscle was tight and tender. I was certain that the intense pain in my stomach was due to a pair of scissors forgotten by the surgeon and that the lump they'd discovered on my leg was a cancer so malignant that I'd be dead by nightfall. I needed specialists—the best the medical profession had to offer, not the attention and unpredictable attacks of a schizophrenic biker chick who had more tattoos than teeth and probably got pregnant in the fourth grade.

"Where the hell do you get off talking to me like that? You ain't no fucking doctor or nurse. I'll bet you don't even know how to spell *hospital*. So while I go back to bed why don't you be a good little aide or waitress or whatever the fuck you're inadequately trained for and go get me some coffee and a jelly donut." I turned and headed back to my bed half expecting my skull to be crushed in with a chair. Instead, she jumped in front of me and again stood with her face right in mine.

"Dallas," she said less sweetly, "don't run anymore. You can't. You don't have the time. This body can't take it anymore. You won't have another chance at recovery. This is it." There were tears in her eyes and a note of urgency in her voice. This one was very clever. But even though it was clear that she'd won, that within minutes I'd be sitting in her fucking group, I wasn't going to make it easy for her.

"Look, there's no point . . . there's no coming back. I've been doing shit so long I turned into it. Don't waste your time on me. I'm not worth it and someone will probably get hurt," I said.

"I know you're worth it," she said. "You've got to let others, let me, care for you until you learn to care for yourself." She took my hand.

"That's not possible after the shit I've done. No one could care about me, and anyone who says they do is lying or uninformed." I let go her hand and turned away. The brain was warming up. She wanted drama, I could easily oblige. It meant nothing to me, all I cared about was getting the maximum effect.

"Self pity is a beautiful thing," she said, applauding to my back. "And you're very good at it. Let me show you something." I turned as she was rolling up the sleeves of her shirt, revealing thin white arms, littered with scars. She pointed to several deep ones on her wrists.

"Suicide attempts. Ages twelve, thirteen, twenty-five, and this one, the deepest, three years ago," she said.

I bared my arms and pointed to the scars of old needle-induced abscesses, and then hiked up my shirt to show her my bandages. "And at least twenty overdoses. Ten on purpose," I said.

"I had twice that," she said as she hoisted up her T-shirt, revealing a large, mid-abdominal scar. "Hysterectomy. Age twenty-one. I was turning tricks for drugs and got so infected, taking it out was the only way to save my life."

I lifted my shirt again and showed my laparotomy scar. "Car accident. Hit by a drunk driver. Killed one of my best friends. Paralyzed another," I said.

She took off her boots and rolled up her jeans to reveal many tiny, old scars. "Drunk stepfather. Burned me with cigarettes until I was old enough to rape." I felt embarrassed and sad and outdone. I had a few more scars but could tell from the look on her face that she hadn't even gotten warmed up yet.

"Let's go to group," I said.

We walked more slowly than we had to down the long, gray hallway to the detox unit. I knew she didn't buy for a minute that I had any physical pain at all, but the truth was my belly did hurt and I was feeling very nervous and ambivalent. If I'd been physically able, I would have tried again to jump out a window and escape.

The clinic ran a clean, highly thought of program with a reputation for a good staff and a respectable success rate. I'd been transferred there after I got caught AWOL—I'd slipped out the window practically into the arms of an orderly—and was now to begin the first phase of their recovery program. Until I was detoxed I would reside with the other detoxers in a large circular room at the end of this hall known as "The

Fishbowl," and from there I'd move onto the ward. It would be at least a thirty-day stay, and I hadn't stayed anywhere for thirty days in a decade. I knew that what Candy and Trudy and Dr. Fremont and everyone who knew me said was true, that this was my last chance, but I found the thought of giving up my last friend, drugs, impossible to comprehend.

The trip down the hall was anything but dull—peopled with characters who ranged from those outrageously acting out to those who seemed barely alive. It was reminiscent of a hospital hallway I'd been in on a seventy-two-hour hold, in a locked psych ward where the population was, in general, much more profoundly disturbed than this bunch of junkies pissed about being separated from their dope.

"I've got a cig-a-rette," the heavy young man said in a singsong voice. He was waving a lit cigarette, trailing the smoke through the air like a child would fly a toy airplane.

"Dallas Taylor, meet Brian Wilson," said the large black psych ward tech as he shut the heavy iron gate behind us.

I had just voluntarily committed myself to the psych ward of Brotman Hospital. I was there because I had broken into my girlfriend's apartment and destroyed the place because she wasn't home. In the process something heavy had fallen on one of my fingers—it was broken at the base of the nail and the bone was sticking out—so I went to the Emergency Room at Brotman. I was afraid things would get out of hand so I talked to the E.R. doctor and he agreed that I should sign myself in. After shooting me up with Valium, he arranged for me to be escorted up to the third floor, and now as I looked around me I realized that I had made a serious mistake. I was trapped. Still, between the Valium and the IV

Demerol, I wasn't feeling particularly anxious; in fact, I didn't give a fuck where I was.

"My songs are like a strawberry milkshake," Brian confided to me. He was standing in the middle of the hallway, barefoot, wearing nothing but a loose hospital gown which was open in the back. I was too stoned to be open-mouthed but the thought did cross my mind that this butt-naked wild-eyed loon was one of the world's premier genius songwriters, composer of some of the most beautiful and sensitive music the Beach Boys—or for that matter anyone—had ever performed. It was too difficult to think about.

"Don't talk to the chicks," Brian said, "they're evil and they'll steal your soul. Just stay close to me and you'll be all right."

I was called over to my room because a doctor had come up about the results of my x-rays. "We're going to operate on that finger now," the doctor said. "You've broken it really badly and it needs a pin. We're going to have to stick a wire under your fingernail and wire it into the bone to hold it together."

Now I was feeling a little panicked. "Cool," I replied. "Do I get more dope? I'll need more for the pain, a lot more. I'm a junkie you know, so I need more than most people."

"Sure you'll get more dope, Dallas," he said, not unkindly. "You'll be fine, son."

I opened my eyes as wide as I could, trying to give him a puppy-dog look to get empathy and more drugs. But inside I was thinking, "You dick!" I hate tolerant people.

Psych had its own recovery area and as I came to after the surgery, I saw Brian standing over me. He was wearing a stethoscope and was listening to his own heartbeat. "Gotta make sure it still works," he said.

***

My middle finger had a huge bandage on it. "Great," I thought, "what a perfect thing. A big 'fuck you' to the world."

"Fuck you!" I said to no one in particular, as I waved it around.

As we threaded our way down to the Fishbowl, Candy explained a few things to me: after I was detoxed, I'd be transferred to a double room; I would be part of a group that consisted of four patients, herself, and an aide; she would be in charge of running my group and only one other and she could easily keep tabs on eight people. I took a deep breath as we reached the doorway and entered.

The Fishbowl was large and crowded with beds and patients and nurses and I felt claustrophobic. Candy introduced me to the rat-faced head nurse, who gave off extremely unpleasant vibes, and her second-in-command, a young nellie gay black man named Lenny, who was instantly likeable. Lenny would also be Candy's aide in our group. Without stopping, Candy took me to a small area away from the nurses where two women and two men wearing hospital pajamas and bathrobes were waiting for us. We sat in the two empty chairs and Candy instructed us all to pull into a circle. Everyone but the boy next to me responded. He was a Hispanic teenager who sat erect but showed no other sign of life. Candy and the other guy, a hippie, moved him in his chair.

The linoleum felt cold through my slippers and the lights were too bright and revealing. I hadn't let myself be seen in this kind of light in years and obviously neither had any of the other corpses sitting around me. A curtain was pulled so that we might have some privacy and Candy began by introducing herself, and then told us to do the same.

"I'm not really a drug addict," a small, dark-haired woman named Jill said in a very nasal voice. "I'm anorexic and bulimic and just use cocaine to keep my weight down." With prompting she then admitted that she'd been snorting coke for two years and had recently been fired from her job as a stewardess because of erratic behavior and absenteeism. She was thin and very pale with a tiny nose that always ran and an all-American girl face. She was clearly terrified of us and not at all comfortable talking about herself.

"Did you leave anything out?" Candy asked before moving on, obviously already knowing the answer.

"Oh, yeah. I also abuse laxatives. So even if I ask, don't give me any," she said, red with embarrassment.

"And to think I was just about to offer you one," said the hippie, who was seated on my right. "Perhaps you'd like a breath mint instead?" He was about my age with long, unwashed hair that was tied back with a rawhide strap and round, wire-rimmed spectacles with greasy lenses. He had many sores on his skinny arms and long fingernails with dirt caked hard underneath.

"Are you listening, darling?" he continued. "This little Gidget gets high off sitting on the crapper. Isn't that funny?" He directed this toward a woman sitting opposite him who appeared to find that there was not much funny in life, least of all him. She looked forty and mean. She had a long face, thin lips, and big eyes which stared intently at whomever spoke, as though she were hard of hearing or having difficulty comprehending the language.

"And what funny stuff were you doing, John, to land yourself in here?" asked Candy.

"Heroin," he said proudly, "the drug of enlightenment." His eyes were as drab gray as the room and the day, and his smile revealed teeth covered with pond scum. He sat forward with his hands on his knees and appeared on the edge of falling face first. An educated, cynical, and dignified junkie with very little living left in him.

"I was kidding, of course, about the crapper," he said to a mortified Jill. "I didn't mean anything. I never do. Ask my loving wife, Elaine." Elaine continued to glare at him with even less love than humor, but she remained tight-lipped.

"Darling," he continued to Elaine, "you're a bulimic, aren't you? I mean, you certainly spend a great deal of time vomiting, and God knows, you're very good at it. Perhaps you'd care, at this juncture, to say something."

"Leave me the fuck out of this!" she suddenly barked in a hoarse voice. She started opening and closing her fists and turned her lethal stare on Candy.

"We're court-ordered," said John. "If we don't complete this program, we lose our daughter and Elaine goes directly to jail."

"It's not fair!" screamed Elaine, suddenly drenched in tears. "It's just not fair!"

"Ah, but what in life is?" said John. "A corrupt society is never just, no matter how well-intentioned. Nor can a mother be. This is my sixth rehab and her tenth. Is that right, lambchop? Is this number ten or eleven?"

"Make him shut up!" Elaine screamed at Candy. "Shut his evil mouth or I'll shut it for him."

"She gets a little testy when she's withdrawing and I'm her favorite target. Here you go, darling," he said pointing to his cheek. "Plant one right here. You'll feel much better." Elaine bolted from her chair and before she could be stopped, slapped John so hard it knocked him out of his seat and sent his glasses flying into the curtain. Candy was up in a second, and sure enough, was all over Elaine like the promised ugly rash.

"*No!*" screamed Candy. "There will be no hitting in my group! Got it? You sit down now and if you try that again, sister, you're out of here and your ass is in jail!" Elaine meekly helped John to his seat and returned to hers.

It was exciting to see Candy lose her cool and I resented Elaine for having accomplished this before me. I had always been the worst patient wherever I was and was not ready to relinquish that distinction without a fight. The only way to top her, however, would be to actually get thrown out of group and, though I was still physically and mentally impaired, I felt I could probably succeed in this by relying on instinct alone. I was gifted at getting thrown out of places. There wasn't a maitre d', record executive, or close friend within a thousand miles who hadn't thrown me out at some time or another in the past decade. One of my more recent seventy-two-hour holds had lasted all of thirty-six hours, at which time the hospital staff politely gave me back my belongings and suggested that I get the hell out. I wasn't sure about going that far this time, at least not today. I was feeling tired and starting to think only about my next pain shot.

When John's spectacles had bounced off the curtain they had landed in the frozen teenager's lap. Jill timidly retrieved them and handed them back to John.

"There," said John, "now don't we all feel better that we've got that behind us? Who's next?"

Elaine actually looked less tense and appeared to be working on a smile. Jill looked about ready to jump under her chair. John's face was starting to swell.

"Paolo, tell us why you're here," said Candy to the teenager. He was obviously a gang member with his black hair combed back hair-net style and his amateur tattoo, the tears and crosses of someone who has done time in jail. He sat with his arms and legs folded and his eyes at half-mast. He hadn't moved since we sat down.

"Paolo," Candy continued with understanding in her voice, "where are you right now? What's the name of this place?" She reached over and shook his knee. Paolo's expression finally changed then. He appeared puzzled and started looking around him. What I originally took for a street attitude now appeared to be brain damage.

"Paolo is here for PCP abuse. Aren't you Paolo?" Candy said, answering for him. "His mother and girlfriend brought him in. They say he's been like this for almost a week."

"Good shit," I said, warming up for my turn.

"Don't worry, Paolo, things will clear up. It's going to take time, but don't worry," Candy said.

"Heads of lettuce don't worry," I said. "This boy is gone."

"Why would anyone touch that stuff?" asked Jill.

"No brain, no pain," said Elaine.

"But pumpkin, that's never been true for you," said John.

"If this dude does wake up, is he going to kill us?" I asked.

"Why would you care, Dallas?" Candy said. "We'll come back to Paolo when he's feeling better. You go ahead, Dallas."

"What do you mean, 'Why would you care?' What kind of shit is that?" I said. My head was pounding and all I could think of about was my Demerol and the shape of the syringe they would bring it in, in less than twenty-nine minutes.

"You're here because you want to die. What difference does it make, now?" she asked.

"You know, you'd be prettier outside if you were prettier inside. You're a cruel person," I said.

"Honesty is not cruel," she said, completely unshaken.

"And so fucking self-righteous," I said. "How could you expect us to open up to someone like you?"

"Please try," she said.

"Wrong day, wrong place, wrong person," I said. "I've got no fucking interest in explaining myself to these psychos. How the fuck could these nuts help me? I need people who know what they're doing, not this amateurish AA verbal-diarrhea bullshit. Get me a nurse so I can go back to bed."

Candy narrowed her eyes and crossed her arms. She was choosing her next move. I needed a more vicious personal attack to disarm her.

"And don't try the soft-spoken, seductive thing on me anymore. You're too old and wrinkled for that crap."

She sat silently and then she wrenched her face into a mask of embarrassment and sadness.

"And don't sit there and pretend you're sad and wait for someone to defend you. That won't work either," I said.

"You're a very unpleasant man," said John.

"Now that is rich, coming from you," I said. "How long have you been torturing your old lady? How much longer before you drive her to an overdose or force her to kill you? You're more than unpleasant, man, you're evil. And *you* are going to help me?"

"We see first in others what we fear most in ourselves," John said. "By watching me, maybe I can help you see all the evil things you do to your wife."

"Leave her out of this! I'm nothing like you! We don't do this kind of shit to each other. We love each other." The scene in the kitchen flashed before my eyes.

"Tell us what happened, Dallas. You need to talk about it," she said. Once more, I thought, just one more attack and then she'll leave me alone for good.

"Why don't you tell us what happened on the streets when you were fucking for drugs?" I said. "Did you fuck Mexican vegetables like this dude here? How does it feel to be a sterile, washed-up old hag? Tell us. You need to talk about it." The group was dead silent and I could feel their eyes on me and their hatred.

"Does he have to be in this group?" asked Elaine. "Couldn't we like, let him go to his room or home or to hell or something?"

"It doesn't feel good," Candy slowly said, "and that's why I'm sitting here. Take a look at my life and learn what not to do. Learn from my mistakes and don't end up like me."

"It'll be tough being in a place like this with someone so mean," said Jill.

"Oh, no. Look at him! Listen to him! He's not mean, he's lonely," Candy said, starting to cry.

"Don't start with the tears. . . . Nobody here will believe tears," I said.

"You're just like my daughter," said Elaine. "You need a lot of attention. Any kind of attention. If you don't get it being good then you get it being bad. Anything is better than being ignored."

"You must have been very deprived as a child," John said.

"That's bullshit. How the fuck would you know? Mind your own business," I said.

"You see a lot in six hospitalizations," he said.

"Try cleaning them fucking eyeglasses once a year or so and you'll see that this is all bullshit and it ain't going to work on me," I said.

"I get it! He could also be testing us," Jill said. "He could be trying to push us away to see if we keep coming back. I used to do that. I guess I still do."

"Stay out of this Gidget," I said.

"Or he could be scared," said Elaine. "You back a dog into a corner and he bites."

"Or maybe, just maybe, I'm a nasty prick. Has anyone thought of that? Maybe the only motivation is hatred. Maybe I derive pleasure from other people's suffering."

"That's not even close to the truth," Candy said. She stood, walked over, and put her arms around me. She hugged me gently and softly sobbed.

"I don't buy this! This is pure manipulation! This won't work on me."

"I know," she said, "and that's what's so sad. You're too clever and burned and broken. I don't think there's anything we can do."

"What do you mean?" I said. "Oh, I get it, reverse psychology. By telling me this you think I'll be forced to go the distance just to prove you wrong. Right? *Wrong!* I'll do what I want and it'll have nothing to do with you! Stop crying! *Stop!*"

I pinched her on the arm like she'd done to me earlier in the hope that she'd respond similarly or that, at the very least, she'd laugh, but she didn't. Her tears were real and unless she was a very good actress, they were for me. Perhaps she could see into the future and knew there was no hope. I'd known that for years but I didn't like having it confirmed. I fought off an urge to run and sat there quite still, unable to advance or retreat, as she held me and gently rocked.

The circle was silent for what seemed a very long time until Paolo came suddenly alive. He smiled and snapped his fingers as if a light had just been turned on inside.

"The hospital," he said. "I'm in the hospital. . . ."

5

Wish Upon a Star

I open my eyes and I see Betty, my wife, smiling and saying, "It's the hospital, you're in the hospital. The surgery went fine." I have no idea what she's talking about and struggle to get up so I can go find my Harley and get the hell out of wherever the hell we are.

Then two nurses tighten the restraints on my wrists and a third puts something into my IV. I am overwhelmed by this act of treachery and try to tell Betty that I want a divorce when I realize there is a tube in my throat. I can't even begin to think what evil purpose this is serving and I strain to pull it out but can't. For no apparent reason these people have decided to hold me down and kill me. As the poison takes effect and I start to die, I memorize the faces of everyone in the room and swear revenge. Then, as I slip back into unconsciousness their faces merge with others as more memories come into view.

A few months before I discovered the drums, I had became obsessed with cars. In the late fifties, the Corvette

Sting Ray was the vehicle of choice of every teenager in San Antonio and I cut out pictures of them from magazines, collected brochures from the Chevy dealership, and rode my bike through expensive neighborhoods looking for one parked in the driveway. If no one was around, I'd touch it.

My mother was going through one of her periods of sadness and withdrawal and she was spending most of her time in the house. My grandfather explained that she had high blood pressure and so had to take medicine which made her tired, but I was beginning to suspect that she stayed in bed all day because she had nothing to get up for. My grandmother, thinking I was lonely and in need of a father figure, persuaded a trusted family friend we'll call Bill to spend some time with me. Bill, about six years older than I was, looked like Roy Orbison. He usually brought a friend with him on the Saturday afternoons we spent together and they'd take me to some deserted house or vacant lot and force me to have sex with them. Then they'd drop me off back home where my grandmother would feed me cookies and tell me how lucky I was to have a friend like Bill. I'd go back to my room, convinced that I was a homosexual, and after throwing up everything I'd just eaten, I'd rearrange my Corvette collection and dream of driving away.

We moved from the little house on Drexel Avenue to a duplex in a better neighborhood in the city when the state bought the house because it needed the land for a freeway. I had my own room, and I liked that, although at times, even if I was too old to admit it, I missed the comfort of sharing a room with my mother and falling asleep to the rhythm of her breathing.

My grandparents lived in the adjoining apartment. Shortly after we moved my grandfather died and my grandmother became increasingly dependent on my mother, and she would cross over to our side of the house every morning to get us up and make sure we got some breakfast. One morning my grandmother had made toast and eggs and knocked on my mother's door holding her coffee. She raced into my room and grabbed my shoulders, speaking in a mixture of Spanish and English, which I didn't understand. I followed her to my mother's room and when I entered, I knew instantly that something was wrong. It looked exactly the same, clean and frilly, all done in violet—her name was Violet and almost everything she owned was that color. My mother was lying comfortably in the center of the bed, the sheets pulled up to her chin. Her eyes were closed and her skin looked as pale as her hair and as thin as the sheer curtains that billowed at the windows. I touched her hand and cheek. They were cold and firm. I shook her and then put my head to her chest. Never had I heard anything more still and vacant. I felt underneath her pillow for her piece of bread and finding it there, took comfort in knowing that she hadn't choked. My grandmother and I looked at each other and she ran out to get Darlene, who lived across town.

I sat on the bed, holding my mother's hand, and waited for my grandmother to return. For an hour I looked at my mother as I never had before. I tried to memorize her. I touched her cheeks and her small ears and her dark eyebrows, still the warm color her white hair had once been. The veins in her arms and hands were still supple and I took both her hands in my own and tried to rub away the chill. They were always so soft and warm and clean smelling. I let them go only when the ambulance arrived with my grieving grandmother and Darlene. I sat in a chair next to the bed while the ambulance people pronounced my mother dead and I kissed her on the cheek before they wheeled her out of the room. Darlene left to accompany the ambulance to the hospital. The task of making the funeral arrangements fell to her. My grandmother retreated to her side of the house to be alone with her grief. And I ran out the door.

I sat for hours on a hill above the highway watching cars leave the city, like birds flying in formation off to someplace warmer, greener, more peaceful. As the sky grew dark, the line of cars grew more magical, their headlights casting beams of white toward where they were going, their taillight casting red on where they'd been. I imagined myself among them, accelerating into a new world, the speed washing the fear and the dread from my mind, releasing me from the darkness behind. I made up my mind that if I were to go where my mother had gone, then I would go midflight, in a blaze of sparks and lightning like Fricke. I would disintegrate in the white of my headlights, I would not slip peacefully and willingly, as she had into the trailing light of her past.

It was Sunday, another hot, moist day. We had been scheduled to perform on Saturday, but not surprisingly, things were way behind schedule and we finally got a slot for Sunday night. Stephen sat on the edge of the stage watching the crowd and the position of the cameras and lights on the towers. He could have been dreaming of the new world or at least savoring the moment but he appeared detached from his surroundings, his slight movements reminding me of an athlete sizing up the competition at a meet. His face was lean and hard. He squeezed out a half-smile for all of the common folk who made a point of saying hello. The truly famous who greeted him received a handshake or a hug and an invitation to jam together sometime. He spent more time playing off stage than on, usually with people more famous or talented.

Bruce and I wandered around for a while, then settled down with some leg-numbing hashish we'd found at the other end of the stage.

"When's Joplin performing?" a chubby roadie with a red ponytail and motorcycle tattoo asked.

"She's on next," Bruce said, reaching for the pipe.

"She was already on and she was fucking great," said a short Janis look-alike in feathers and silver who was trying to light a spent sparkler.

"That wasn't Joplin," said a man dressed in peach robes with many beads and a very long beard. "That was Grace Slick."

"She's a nice piece. Janis is a pig," said the man with the ponytail.

"You're an asshole," the woman said.

"Who's on now?" asked Bruce, his head too heavy to lift.

"The Who was on yesterday," said the woman. "They've gone Hollywood. Who really wants to see Roger Daltrey's belly button? They're no longer relevant."

"Sha Na Na is irrelevant," said the red ponytail. "Whose stupid fucking idea was it to invite them?"

"They should have asked Janis Ian and Joni Mitchell," said the woman. "This festival is about poems and pain."

"Bunch of buck-toothed warbling women," said the ponytail. "This festival is about revolution with guitars, not guns, and not about 'ice cream castles in the air.' "

"Joni couldn't come," I said. "She's doing *The Dick Cavett Show* and she wouldn't have been able to get out of there in time."

"You're making that up." The woman appeared stunned. "She would never sell out like that."

"She ain't selling out," said Bruce to the sky. "She's making a career."

"She doesn't care about a career!" said the woman. "I'm sure she's here or on her way or visiting someone in a hospital or something."

"That's Stephen Stills," said the man in peach nodding towards Stephen. "He's brought a new band here. Isn't he balling Judy Collins?"

"They're all acoustical. Far-out harmonies. I love their vision," said the woman. "He's handsome."

"More fluff," said the ponytail. "You don't break down walls with gooey ballads. They need some fucking backbone. Thank God Hendrix is here. When does he go on?"

"He was already on," said the man in peach. "Loud and mediocre. What he lacks in talent he makes up for in volume."

"That wasn't him," said the man in the ponytail, "that was some other black guy. Crosby, Stills and Nash are my least favorite people from all the groups they came from. They'll never be big."

"You guys are un-fucking-believable! I thought we were supposed to be nonjudgmental," said Bruce trying to stand up. "I thought we were the family of man."

"We are nevertheless entitled to our opinions," said the bearded man, looking at the spotlights through a glass ball. He held a joint up to Bruce's face.

"This allows us not to act on them, not to try to force them down others' throats. This is the difference. This will bring peace to the world." Bruce was swaying like a mast in a storm.

I hit my legs to bring life back to them and tried in vain to stand and take his side. They reminded me of my uncles, who'd sit on the front porch in the evenings, putting down everything that walked by and drinking so much gin they'd either fall asleep or off the porch. I searched my mind for something devastatingly cutting to say.

"You guys make me puke," was the only thing that came to mind. "Who gives a rat's ass about your fucking opinions? You're nobodies. I'll bet none of you ever even sat in a Porsche!" I reached for the joint that was coming my way and the ponytail held it back. The three exchanged glances and the one in peach spoke.

"I think there is something that we all agree on. You're bringing us down."

"Come on, Bruce, I think we've been uninvited," I said.

"Story of my life," he said, trying to pick out a direction. He grabbed my arms and hoisted me on his back like a sack. I pointed toward Stephen and he started dragging me around the periphery of the stage. Midstage we passed someone dragging Keith Moon in the opposite direction.

"This happens a lot to drummers?" Bruce asked me.

"All the time. We sit so much our legs rot. Put me down next to Stephen. Let's show those nothings that we're somebody."

I knew Keith and we exchanged nods. I'd met him through Laura, at the age of sixteen she "knew" more musicians than I'd met. I admired everything about Keith, who was famous for wildly outrageous stunts like driving a limo into the pool of the Beverly Wilshire Hotel, tossing his drum set into the audience, and trashing rooms in some of the finest hotels in the world. Of course I was jealous that he was a better drummer than I was and because he was sleeping with

Laura but we became friends in spite of that. He was so funny and crazy and childlike and charming that if I were a girl, I would have fucked him, too. When I was hanging out with Keith I tried my best to keep up with him, so it shocked me when he said, "Dallas, you'd better slow down. You do way too much coke. You're too crazy for me, mate." He told me this at the end of a wild visit to his house that had lasted three days and nights. When he died, I wasn't surprised, but I wondered why I was still alive.

Watching the world from my view over Bruce's shoulder, I decided that this was the perfect way to go through life. The only effort required of me was in choosing a general direction. The work was entirely the responsibility of someone else. It struck me that ever since I'd met Stephen, our relationship had been variations on this theme. His drive, his ambition, his power would take me where I wanted to go and his talent would force me to be the best I could be. Bruce dragged me over the electrical cables, muddy feet, unused two-by-fours, and an entire organic pizza, and stopped directly in front of Stephen.

"How's it look, Chief?" I asked, feeling suddenly embarrassed.

"Are you going to be able to play?" he asked, smiling but with an edge in his voice.

"Ambulation appears to be the only problem," I said, struggling to stand. "The arms never let me down."

Stephen took my arms and slid me to a sitting position next to him. Bruce sat on my other side. He was still having problems stabilizing his head.

"It looks like we've got a good slot after all," Stephen said. "Everyone's going to be watching us." Stephen looked at Paul Kantner sitting with Jerry Garcia and Joe McDonald and appeared worried. I looked out toward the audience and saw in the growing darkness, a million Cheshire cat eyes staring at us. They were all glowing with the reflection of the stage lights and the sunset and every few seconds one or two would take to the air like fireflies.

"Oh, oh," I said, unsure if I'd accidentally taken a hallucinogen or if it was just my preperformance freak out.

"We can handle it," Stephen said with a hint of uncertainty. He was looking at a group of reporters who were standing at the front of the stage talking to Bill Graham. I grabbed Bruce's head and pulled it up by the hair so that he was looking at the audience with us.

"Do you see flying glowing eyeballs?" I whispered in his ear.

"Sparklers and cigarettes," he said definitively. I let go of his hair and his head dropped back down toward the stage.

"Ought to get that fixed," said Crosby, walking up behind us. He was eating an apple, breathing heavily from some kind of rush, and was looking for someone. It was still hot and muggy and the air was thick with the odors of cooking food and hashish and David was wearing a fur jacket. With his long hair and handlebar mustache he looked like a bear or a lost arctic explorer.

John Sebastian walked up behind him and put his arm on his shoulder. Crosby responded by offering him a bite of his apple.

"You gotta like Crosby," whispered Bruce to the air directly above him. "He is what he is. A nice, honest, thoroughly mellow fat man." I did like David, in fact, idolized him. His easy manner inspired trust and he ignored most of the pettiness that surrounded him. He had a self-assurance that came from having been successful early and the smile of a mischievous five year old, which drove women crazy. I shared hot tubs and women and drugs with him as often as I could, and I followed him around like a little brother, stealing lines and looks and moves. David's smile was the most difficult thing to perfect and for some reason, my version usually had the exact opposite effect on women. Rather than cute, they found it demonic and responded with a gasp.

"He's not fat," I said to Bruce, feeling a roll of flesh above my belt.

"Forgive me," Bruce said. "Chubby." I looked up at David looking at the crowd and then looked at the roadies and groupies and other band members surrounding the stage, all looking at him. He had been a Byrd. He was rock royalty.

"Someday people are going to look at me like that," I said to Bruce.

John and David were filling the silence from a break in the show between bands with a harmony. They sang two lines of some old song that I didn't know into a brisk wind that wouldn't carry it more than five feet, took two last bites of the apple, and then hopped off the stage and took off in the direction of the crowd.

"Let's go!" I said to Bruce, eager to get away from Stephen and to watch David and John in action.

"Can't be done," he said, not even trying to move. "I believe my karma wants me right here."

"Well, mine says move on and find something to make these legs and thoughts move easier," I said.

Bracing myself on a speaker and a roadie's legs, I made it to my feet and tried to focus in the direction David had gone. Drummers were supposed to be reckless and wasted but not before they were legends, and particularly not before the biggest performance of their life, so I avoided Stephen by walking behind him and to the right, and stumbled toward the end of the stage with my head down, pretending that I'd lost something. I walked for what seemed a good fifteen minutes, and then I looked up and noticed that I'd moved about three feet. Then I saw Grace Slick sitting on a speaker straight ahead of me, looking at me as if I were a madman. She was a star and beautiful and definitely one of the women of the world that I wanted most to impress, and walking like a two year old who had just shit in his pants was not going to do it. If I turned away or stopped and pretended to look at something, I was sure to lose David and John, so I decided to continue forward, however unsteadily, with my head up, making sure that my feet moved at a normal rate. I took one step, tripped over a power cable, and somersaulted out of control until I came to rest with a thud at the front of the speaker Grace was sitting on. I looked up and saw that she'd lifted her feet to avoid being hit and was staring down at me in disbelief.

"So, you want to go out?" I asked her. She started to laugh, then she slid off the speaker, carefully lowering her feet to avoid stepping on me. She stood and walked quickly away, still laughing, never looking back, the white Indian fringe on her low-cut top disappearing with unbelievable speed into the stage crowd.

"You must be a big hit with the ladies," I heard a voice say. I turned to see a pretty teenage girl pointing a camera at me.

"Smile!" she said as the flash went off, so completely blinding me that I missed the edge of the stage and fell off, landing at her feet.

"Do you bruise easily?" she asked, helping me get up.

"Not before this moment," I said trying to get a good look at her. She was as tall as I was, thin, wearing jeans and a handkerchief halter top. A big leather purse was hanging from her shoulder. "But no telling now. My body ain't exactly behaving normally today. Who are you?"

"Kathy," she said, smiling with very big, perfect teeth. "What's yours?" She had long, dark hair, tanned, flawless skin, and gold earrings. She looked exactly like Grace Slick must have when she was fifteen.

"We'll get to that," I said, reaching for her arm. "How old are you?"

"Why?" she said, angrily. "I'm not a groupie. I'm a photographer."

"Oh," I said. "Help me walk around and I'll get you some great photographs." I gave her my most mischievous Crosby-like smile.

"Are you into Satanism or something?" she asked.

"That's my mischievous grin," I said. "Hmmm, do you have any older sisters?"

"No, only large, older brothers," she said pulling away her arm.

"OK. I'm looking for two friends of mine: John Sebastian and David Crosby. You help me find them and you'll get lots of pictures," I said.

"Of who?" she asked

"They're not enough? They're big stars!" I said.

"Do you know Roger Daltrey or Joe Cocker?" she asked.

"Close personal friends," I lied. "They just went through the crowd, this way." She gave me back her arm and I leaned heavily on it. The crowd was tighter than ever and was very difficult to get through walking side-by-side, so I moved behind her, and steadied myself by putting both hands on her shoulders. She shrugged them off.

"Are you a dirty old man?" she asked, stopping abruptly and turning to face me.

"I'm twenty-one!" I said. "I can't be more than three years older than you. Four? Five? Six?" She nodded when I said "six."

"So are you an experienced fifteen? Like, fifteen going on thirty?" I asked.

"Fifteen going on sixteen," she said. "I'm not kidding you. I came to get photographs — not to get balled by some demonic old man!"

"OK. Got it!" I said. "You help me get through the crowd and I'll help you get your damn pictures. But I am not an old man!" I extended my hand, we shook, and she turned and started pulling me through the crowd. We headed quickly in the general direction of the audience through an obstacle course of hippies sleeping, eating, dancing, juggling, and selling. Kathy was strong and her no-nonsense towing gave me no time for sightseeing.

"I love that song," she said stopping suddenly. "Who sings that?"

"I do," I said. "Crosby, Stills, Nash and Young."

"Which one are you?" she asked.

"The drummer," I said, trying to avoid the next question. I shook her hand to get her started again.

"We're going the wrong way," she said. "We're heading out toward the audience."

"That's where they went," I said.

"It took me two hours to talk my way in here and I'm not going through that again."

"You're with me," I said. "No problem."

"Who are you?" she asked.

"Graham Nash," I said, bowing. She rolled her eyes, threw away my hand, turned and started to walk away. I lunged for her and caught her purse.

"All right, I'm not Graham. My name is Dallas. I'm the drummer in Crosby, Stills, Nash and Young and I don't get any billing, but I am a vital member of the band."

"You got any proof?" she asked.

"Proof?" I said. With no famous friends, album covers, or expensive automobiles close by, I was exactly like every other hippie here. "No," I said. "You'll have to wait and see me perform. We're on in a couple of hours. I'll get you on stage. You can get great pictures from there."

"Fair enough," she said after a second. "Just remember that I've got five big brothers and my father is a cop. Which way?" I pointed in the direction from which we'd come and she whipped me around and we raced back toward the stage.

We traveled for what seemed an hour but had only gone about thirty steps when we ran into Graham walking with Roger Daltrey. Kathy's eyes got as big as Graham's when he looked at her.

"Dallas, my friend, where are you headed and who's this?" he said, reaching for her hand.

"Kathy," I said, sandwiching myself between them. "She's . . . my niece and she's . . . got an infection. I'm taking her to a first aid station."

"That's not true," she said.

"She's very embarrassed about it," I whispered into his ear. "Here! Let me take a picture of the three of you!" I took her camera and she posed girlishly between them, smiling like a five year old standing with Mickey Mouse and Pluto.

"Thanks a lot! Gotta go before the fever gets too high. She gets . . . seizures when that happens," I said pulling her into the safety of the crowd.

"Why'd you do that?" she said angrily.

"Graham's a dirty old man. Old enough to be your father. He fucks every woman he meets. Your father is going to thank me."

"I've never been so embarrassed in my whole life! That was Roger Daltrey!"

"One of the meanest sons of bitches you'll ever meet. Ten seconds more and he would have stolen your purse or stepped on your foot."

"You're lying," she said.

"You're right."

"Why?"

"Because I'm afraid you'll like them better because they're more famous than me." She pulled me to a complete stop and smiled. Suddenly she was no longer a young girl, she was a woman, and her pat on my shoulder was filled with understanding. She tousled my hair and took charge, holding my hand as if I were her child.

We found John's tent by luck and a little instinct and I left her outside with the excuse that the space was filled with drugged-out, sex-fiend roadies. I was hoping there would be someone in there who would have some coke. When I entered I tripped over a pile of pillows and blankets and landed on a suspiciously hard mound. I got lucky. The passed-out woman beneath the pillows was a friend of Guinnevere's, and there was a very good chance that I'd be able to score some coke, which would make me whole again.

"Ow!" she said. I threw the cushions aside, uncovered the sleeping girl, and kissed her on the forehead.

"I'm a star," I said searching for her purse. "Let's do some coke."

"Who are you?" she asked, grabbing the purse to her breast.

"Look at me," I said. "Focus."

She tried. Then she sat up and fished in her pocket for some granny glasses. She put them on and squinted.

"Keith Richard?" she asked.

"Close," I said. "Pete Townsend, actually."

"I've never had you," she said, taking off her halter top with lightning speed, releasing two long eggplant-shaped breasts.

"I'm a bit . . . tired. I'll need some help getting up for this," I said, a little too obscurely. Within seconds she had her hand on my dick and was pulling it like it was a doorknob.

"No!" I said, lifting my eyes from the eggplants and wrenching my dick from her grasp. "I mean cocaine. I need cocaine."

"Oh," she said reaching into her purse. She pulled out a long, clear glass test tube sealed with a black rubber stopper filled with what must have been several ounces of the white powder. "How do you want to do it?" she asked.

"Alone," I said too quickly, and then catching myself, "with you. Let's just snort." I grabbed the tube, popped off the stopper, and covered the large hole with a nostril. Blocking the other with a finger, I inhaled deeply and sucked an unprecedented amount of cocaine up my nose.

"Oh, oh," she said. "This is pure stuff that I get from my cousin in Vietnam. That much can make you forget to breathe."

"I'll be fine," I said, wiping an avalanche of white powder from my nose and lips. "I've been doing downers all day, and anyway, my tolerance is pretty high." The blood vessels in my brain were opening wide and a torrent of fire washed through. My eyes bulged out and I lost feeling in my hands and my feet. "Good shit," I said, standing. "When does God arrive?" I started pacing on the pillows and had to dodge her every time I was within reach.

"Come on, Pete," she said, hiking up her Indian print skirt revealing everything she should have hidden from mankind forever. I shrieked and ran from the tent on a pair of legs that felt a little more nearly like mine but were still almost as uncontrollable as they were before. The cocaine had given them too much strength and steam, taking away their ability to do anything but accelerate.

"Let's go!" I shouted as I passed Kathy and headed toward the stage.

"Where are we going?" she screamed. "Slow down!"

"Can't!" I called over my shoulder. "Too much to see!" The people around me blurred and I could barely hear the music over my own heartbeat.

"What's wrong with you?" Kathy asked. She had caught up with me and was holding onto my arm.

"Fast cars," I said. "Speed. Slow down and you die. Take your foot off the accelerator and something black catches up and buries you." I was navigating the hippie jungle with the numbness and agility of a great cat running for its life or searching for food. I could feel Kathy's small hand grabbing mine about a mile away, pulling weakly to get me to slow down.

"Like, are you on a drug or something?" she asked.

"Medicine, soul food," I shouted.

"Give me some!" she said. "I've never tried drugs. I want to do everything—once." I stopped and turned and tried to focus on her. My eyes fluttered and wavered and then

responded like the polished and powerful lenses of a tele-
scope and I saw Kathy as if for the first time. Her angles and
colors were almost inhumanly perfect and her tan, fresh body
was more delicate than I thought possible. I walked slowly
toward her, releasing her hand so that she wouldn't feel
trapped, and stopped directly in front of her. My mind's
sudden clarity perceived a new receptiveness tempered by a
good deal of fear, so instead of kissing her, I crossed the six
inches between our faces only to smell her hair and gently
caress the side of her neck. Her hair smelled of an herbal
shampoo and her neck stiffened but she didn't withdraw. I
pinched her cheek to allay her fear and took her back to the
tent where the cocaine monster still lurked in her sea of
pillows. I would teach Kathy about drugs and love and be the
first to open her eyes to this dawn of a new day.

"Move it!" I yelled at people on our way out of the tent.
"Coming through!"

"Slow down!" Kathy screamed at me. "We're missing
lots of beautiful possibilities."

"The secret is in speed!" I shouted over my shoulder to
her. "Possibilities come from speed."

She pulled me to a stop and pointed at a group of people
five feet away. The second big snort that I'd just done with her
was clearly overkill, and I had to find something to cut it or I'd
never be able to get it up for her or play for the crowd.

"It's Jimi Hendrix!" she said with awe and caution.
Then she added, "You don't look good. Are you all right?"

"I think I just did a little too much. I'm feeling a little
anxious and out of control."

"Really? I feel wonderful!" she said pulling me toward
her. "How can you have too much of this feeling?"

"Yeah, well, pain's always hiding somewhere in pleasure. I just need something to take the edge off. A 'lude or a couple bottles of wine."

"How long before you go on?" she asked, twirling in a circle while staring up at the stars.

"Good point! No 'ludes. I've got to play any minute. Any minute? Shit!" I ran toward the stage and stopped after three steps when I saw David walking toward the audience with three women. Relieved, I turned back to Kathy and saw that she was gone. Panic took over until I felt her jump on my back and grab me playfully around the neck.

"I can't believe how much fun this is! My father said drugs would drive me crazy," she said, laughing. "And I am! I'm crazy about everything! Especially you. You are so cute I can't stand it." She kicked me like she would a horse and pointed toward a grassy area away from the stage. I let her down when we were well away from the foot traffic and she grabbed my leg and pulled me down on top of her.

"It's amazing! Ten minutes ago I was afraid you were going to kiss me and now I'm afraid you won't." I held her chin and kissed her lightly and rolled over on my back. I was too wired to be romantic or tender and even I wasn't selfish enough to make her first experience mechanical and unmemorable.

"You're sweating pretty badly. Should we find a doctor or something?" she asked.

"Nah. If I stop breathing, then maybe, but not now. I guess I'm pretty nervous about going on."

"Is that it?" she said, smiling and putting her arm over my chest. "You're going to be fine. Terrific. And even if you're not, hardly anybody is listening anyway. People only come to rock concerts for the experience. The music doesn't matter."

"My music matters . . . wait till you hear me play! Man, we make sounds that no one has ever heard before. I'm serious! Have you heard our album?"

"Sorry, just the one song," she said, shaking her head.

"It's fucking great! No shit. Stephen Stills is basically the leader, and there ain't nothing he can't play. He may be cheap and he may be mean sometimes, but he is the best all-around musician I've ever seen. And then there's Graham who probably has the best voice for harmony in the whole world, and David who was a fucking Byrd, for chrissakes! Add to that Neil Young, who writes the best songs, and my percussion and, well, just hold on to your fucking hat! It's very definitely happening."

She rubbed my chest and stared at me with a puzzled smile. "You sound just like a kid. I guess you're really not too much older than me after all."

"Is that some kind of put-down?" I asked. I felt my tension ease a bit, but I wasn't sure if it was due to having just convinced myself of the inevitability of CSN's acceptance by the rock world or because the coke had stopped producing so much static.

"Not at all," she said taking the lens cap off her camera and pointing it at me. "You finally seem real. You ought to work on your first impression."

"Shit!" I said, suddenly too anxious to sit. "You had to say 'first impression'! We could get slaughtered by the critics tonight! We never rehearse! We get together and fuck around and get fucked up! And now that Young is in the band, anything could happen on the damned stage! He and Stills could fucking beat each other over the heads with their guitars! Too much could go wrong. What if the sound is fucked up and they can't hear my drums? What if the lights aren't working and they leave me out? Man, I need a downer. That's what I need. Let's go get some 'ludes and some wine. Shit! We're too close to going on! I've got to stay like this! I've got to stay like this!"

"Maybe you didn't do enough. I mean, I can't believe how mellow I am. How can you tell if you've done too little or too much?"

"Your body gives you little hints. Like right now, I'm sweating like I'm on fire and if my heart beats any faster, there's a good chance it may explode."

"Why don't we use up some of that excess energy, naturally?" she said. She snapped a photo of me, and then let the camera dangle from her neck. She patted the ground next to her and held open her arms.

"What if Stephen thinks I'm too wasted to play and he's replacing me? He's more worried about how we're going to do than anyone. If I were him, I'd replace me. That's what he's doing. He's going from tent to tent right now looking for someone to take my place. The fucking traitor. He's like my brother and he's doing this to me!"

She reached up and grabbed my pants pockets and pulled me to the ground next to her.

"You've got to relax," she said. I was too convinced of the betrayal being perpetrated and struggled to get back up to pace. Like a gymnast, she swung a leg around and sat on my chest.

"Let me up!" I said. "You don't know what I'm talking about!"

"Neither do you," she said, expertly shifting her weight, making it impossible to move her. "You're getting worked up about nothing."

"Right!" I said. "I've got to keep something going or nothing will take over. I'm not as good as they are! I need them! They don't need me!"

"Then why didn't they get someone else before this? This is their big night, right? They're going to bring along a shitty drummer when they could have anyone in the world they want? You're way too insecure. Did you parents beat you when you were a baby?"

"I'm really too anxious for this. You've got to get off. I can't breathe." She leaned over and grabbed a stick lying in the grass.

"I'll use this to keep you from swallowing your tongue," she said. I arched my back and rocked from side to side but I couldn't move her. She rode me like a rodeo trophy winner. "Are you ticklish?" she asked, sensing the truth and not waiting for my lie. She grabbed at the sides of my belly and my panic grew uncontrollable. I kicked and heaved and had to stop myself from biting her arm, which was within easy range. Then I was laughing and shrieking and roaring. When my hysteria had peaked, she stopped, and I was all done in, completely drained of panic and paranoia.

"Feel better?" she asked, her long hair brushing against my face.

"Yes," I said, genuinely surprised. I really do."

"I do this for my little brother. Keeps him from getting kicked out of school or murdering someone. There's also something good about surrender, but I haven't figured that part out yet." She let go of my arms and tied her hair behind her neck with a leather strap. She then playfully tousled my hair and leaned down, kissing me lightly on the lips.

"Do you do that for your little brother, too?" I asked, beginning to feel comfortable.

"If he really doesn't want me to. That's the only time to kiss a little brother. But never on the lips. Only here," she said, giving me a sloppy kiss on the cheek. She swung her leg around and lay in the grass next to me. "Look! Even with the lights you can still see some stars!" she said, putting her head against my shoulder and her hands around my arm. I fought off a very strong impulse to take the next step. The wrestling had almost completely taken the edge off but it was too soon to tell if it would last.

"Make a wish," she said.

"I don't believe in those stars," I said sitting up. "I believe in these kind of stars." I motioned toward the stage.

"So make a wish on one," she said, still staring into the sky. "We'll see whose wish comes true first." I stood and strained to see a famous face among the shadowed thousands walking in every direction. Unable to find or see anyone familiar, I turned back to Kathy and then I saw Janis Joplin walking through the grass ten feet away. She was with a woman, carrying a drink in her hand and laughing hoarsely.

"There," I said to Kathy, pointing at Joplin. She looked at her and then back at me.

"Make it quick!" she said. "My star's two minutes ahead of yours." I closed my eyes, but I couldn't make up my mind between having Joplin's success, another Ferrari, a Rolex watch, or a house in Malibu, and so I wished for them all and sat back down next to Kathy.

"I'll tell you mine if you'll tell me yours," I said, putting my arm around her. "You might as well. I can tell you for a fact that there's no magic up there. Those stars have been wished dry."

"You go first," she said, giggling and drawing her knees up to her chest.

"No, you!"

"I wished for world peace," she said.

"Me too," I said.

"I can't believe how close I feel to you right now," she said, her face serious. "I feel like I've known you forever, like we're soulmates." She put her hands on my chin and pulled my face to hers. She kissed my cheeks and forehead and eyes and paused before kissing me deeply on the mouth.

6

The Christmas Tree

I must be dead. I can feel nothing, hear nothing, move nothing. I am blind. There is only the vague sense that someone else is breathing for me. This, then, is death . . . or maybe it's brain death. My brain has died and they're keeping the rest of me alive until Betty gives them the go-ahead to cut me loose. But then, why am I thinking, why am I worrying, why this sudden craving for lime Jell-O?

Slowly my senses are returning. I hear a soothing voice and many electronic sounds bumping off each other in the distance. I feel something warm near me, something touching my face softly. The beeps and whistles grow louder, and the voice moves closer. I can feel fingers caressing my lips, my cheeks, my temples. They touch my eyelids, which suddenly open on their own.

It is Betty, my wife. "It's all right," she says, her face very close to mine, "everything went perfectly. You were in there twelve hours, and there were no complications. The doctors said they never had a transplant go so well."

109

She kisses me on the cheek instead of on the lips and then I realize that something big is filling my mouth, my throat. I try to see it but can't. I want to pull it out but my hands won't move.

"It's a breathing tube," Betty says calmly. "They have to keep it in for a little while longer."

"Just to be sure that everything is OK," says a male voice. For the first time I see the room and recognize it as the Intensive Care Unit. The voice belongs to the tall, pale, dark-haired man leading a group of people toward me. They are all dressed in stained green scrubs, and they all look happy. "It went better than we could have hoped," he says. "The liver was healthy and started working right away. You're very lucky."

The faces now all seem familiar and the man's name comes to me as he pulls back the sheet that is covering me. "Not many people wake up this quickly," Dr. Leonard Makowka, the surgeon, says.

I look down to see what he is examining but can recognize nothing as my own. I see all of the bandages and drains and tubes they had prepared us for in the workshops and tours Betty and I had attended prior to the surgery, but they are attached to a pale, monstrously swollen belly that could not be mine. I feel short of breath and I try to breathe faster but the respirator works my lungs at its own pace.

"You'll be off the respirator in a day or so," Dr. Makowka says. "Try not to fight it. Relax, let it do the work."

I look down again and am still in shock. The incision is enormous, only partly covered by bandages. I can see the staples and sutures that are holding my belly together, and it looks as if a giant Mercedes Benz hood ornament has been quilted into my abdomen.

"Are you in pain?" Betty asks, and only then am I aware of it. Now that I am aware, every cell in my body is making its rage known. Dr. Makowka looks at me and then motions someone to put something in my IV.

"We have to be careful with your pain meds," he says. "Most pain medications are metabolized in the liver and your new liver has to feel at home before it gets a lot of work to do."

I look at Betty, who's the only one in the room who knows how much I fear and dread pain. I close my eyes, overwhelmed by the anger of my body at what it has suffered—it is shrieking and on fire. My bladder and bowels are about to explode. I cannot move to reposition myself. I can't even scream because of the respirator, and I cannot, must not, try to manipulate or threaten these doctors into giving me more painkillers because this new liver needs to take root.

Overall the news could not be better. I should be rejoicing, but my body will not allow that. It holds a grudge for all the years of abuse and neglect, and now is the time for payback. Rather than run from this just retribution, I decide not to struggle or wait for the weak shit in my IV to start working. I decide to face my body's rage.

The pain swells and peaks and when I am certain it can get no worse, it does, but then is gone. For a moment I feel victorious, that I have faced down my pain and sent it away. But in the next moment I begin floating downward and I realize the truth as darkness comes.

"I hate Christmas," Elaine said. She took a very long drag on her cigarette.

"That's because you're a nasty, spiteful woman," said Lenny, who was cutting a snowflake out of a piece of orange construction paper. "Once you start letting some niceness into that black heart of yours, you'll be feeling different about Christmas."

It was two days before Christmas, seventy-five degrees outside and the hospital air conditioning wasn't working. Elaine, John, Jill, Lenny, and I sat sweating in the lounge, watching the cheap, dented TV that was hanging from the wall at an odd angle. *It's a Wonderful Life* was on, the scene in which Jimmy Stewart runs his car into the tree and jumps into the river to save Clarence, the guardian angel. "Go fuck yourself, faggot," Elaine said, staring at the TV.

"See!" said Lenny, smiling. "You're getting meaner by the minute." He was right. I'd been here five days and with each day Elaine seemed closer to seriously injuring someone. John said her mood would break after they smuggled in the cocaine this afternoon, but I was convinced that even coke wouldn't do it. What she needed was a good fuck or a quick kick in the teeth, but since that had become my answer for every problem lately, I said nothing.

"This is my big season," John said slowly. "I'm always unusually busy during this time of year." As mean as Elaine was getting, John was getting as depressed. He was thinner and yellower and had stopped even making an attempt at keeping himself clean. He often spoke of the past and avoided talking about his feelings as much as the staff would allow him to. He seemed to have very little hope left in him and I was afraid that he'd die before he found it.

"Ask him what he does for a living," Elaine said. "Go ahead. . . . He makes fucking *wind chimes*. Can you believe it?! No one has used wind chimes in Los Angeles since 1977 and he says Christmas is his busiest time. He sells three, maybe four, of the fucking things from a wooden box that he sets up on Venice beach." She lit another cigarette, forgetting the one smoldering in the ashtray.

"I like wind chimes," said Jill. "They make me feel safe, like I'm a baby in a crib looking up at them." Jill, on the other hand, was becoming more relaxed and self-assured. She had stopped lighting everybody's cigarettes and refilling their styrofoam coffee cups after they'd taken only a sip. She claimed that she had stopped the self-induced vomiting, so the staff no longer watched her after meals, but I knew she was lying. She'd only stopped using the toilet and the sink. I listened at the shower door every day to her choking sounds and could picture the white tile floor covered with bits of food, slowly swirling down the drain. She wore baggy clothes to avoid detection and appeared to have fooled both the staff and herself.

Jill and Candy were the only ones willing to take Elaine on these days. I certainly couldn't. I didn't know myself anymore, so had no side to take. Lenny, Paolo, and Jill said that I'd become paranoid and withdrawn, but Dr. Brett said that this was natural and not to worry about it. The good thing was that I was now actually afraid of dying and of being hurt. If my goal was really to clean up and change my life, then this was definitely progress. Unfortunately I had no idea what my goal was. I just put one foot in front of the other, fantasized about fucking everything that moved, and somehow made it through the day.

"People used to love wind chimes," John said. "They were music made by the wind. They symbolized a harmony with nature. They symbolized a lifestyle of peace, simplicity and truth."

"Well, to me they symbolize a tired old hippie that missed the boat to Silicon Valley," Elaine said. It was clear

---

113

that her impulse had been to say something much more vicious, but at the last second she had managed to rein herself in. Even she saw how bad John was getting and she saved her venom for those who could fight back. She was gunning for Lenny because he was so unflappable and for Jill because she sensed some incipient competition in the "strong woman" department. She stayed away from Candy altogether because we all knew there was no beating her. Candy had revealed herself to be much more than a master manipulator of our little group—she had the strength, intuition, and mission of a lioness defending her litter—and we all competed for her attention. I knew full well that one of the primary reasons for my being involved in the coke smuggling planned for that afternoon was to get more of her time, even though I knew it might backfire, that it might end with my being kicked out. Still, I had to show Candy how truly fucked up I was, how much I needed her, and I clearly hadn't been able to do that with words.

"Are you watching this, Dallas?" Lenny asked. "This is your story. I want you to think about all this before you go sticking yourself with anything ever again." Lenny was dressed in a white polyester shirt and had a corsage composed of Santa's sleigh resting in a snow bank of tinsel pinned on his left shoulder.

I liked Lenny and I trusted him as much as I trusted anyone, but I couldn't tell him that I was unable to concentrate long enough to follow the movie on TV. I was truly afraid that my inability to concentrate and my insomnia and my paranoia and my obsession with sex were not "natural" and "part of withdrawal," but were symptoms of a serious mental illness and I worried that new symptoms would start to appear any moment. I was even more worried that if I did tell anyone,

Dallas Taylor performing with Mannassas at the HIC Arena in Hawaii, 1973. (NEAL PRESTON)

BELOW: *(left to right)* Dallas, Greg Reeves, Graham Nash, Stephen Stills, David Crosby and Neil Young pause long enough for Henry Diltz to capture one of his many images of the band. Los Angeles, 1969. (HENRY DILTZ)

Dallas Taylor—Shady Oak, Studio City, CA 1969. (HENRY DILTZ)

Dallas Taylor's father, Dallas Senior, and his mother Violet.

(DALLAS TAYLOR)

ABOVE: *(left to right)* Greg Reeves, Neil Young, Gary Burdon, Stephen Stills, Dallas Taylor, Graham Nash, and an Unknown gather outside Stills' house in Studio City for a pre-Woodstock rehearsal.

(HENRY DILTZ)

RIGHT: Nash and Taylor rehearsing for Woodstock in Stills' backyard, 1969. (HENRY DILTZ)

BELOW: Crosby, Stills, Nash, and Young performing at Balboa Stadium, San Diego, 1969. (HENRY DILTZ)

ABOVE: Welcome to Woodstock.
(KEN REGAN, CAMERA 5)

LEFT: Eric Clapton in the early '70s.
(UPI/BETTMANN)

Jimi Hendrix, 1970.
(UPI/BETTMANN)

Crosby, Stills, Nash, and
Young performing at the
Santa Barbara Bowl,
1969. (HENRY DILTZ)

John Sebastian *(second from left)* surrounded by members of "The Lovin' Spoonful." (UPI/BETTMANN)

The Woodstock Festival. (KEN REGAN, CAMERA 5)

The Rolling Stones *(left to right)*—Drummer Charlie Watts, Mick
Taylor, lead singer Mick Jagger, guitarist Keith Richards and bass-
player Bill Wyman in 1969. (UPI/BETTMANN)

Janis Joplin, 1970.
(UPI/BETTMANN)

Dallas posing with *(left to right)* Nash, Young, Palmer, Crosby, and Stills on Shady Oak Drive in Studio City, 1969. (HENRY DILTZ)

Dallas drumming.
(HENRY DILTZ)

Dallas Taylor-Stephen Stills solo tour with the Memphis Horns; fondly referred to as the "drunken tour," 1971. (HENRY DILTZ)

BELOW: Leaving Woodstock, the great Love-in of the sixties. (UPI/BETTMANN)

Mama Cass Elliot and Graham Nash. (GARY BURDON AND HENRY DILTZ)

David Crosby, 1969. (HENRY DILTZ)

Dallas Taylor at the Big Sur Celebration of Life Concert, 1969. (HENRY DILTZ)

BELOW: *(left to right)* Neil Young, Greg Reeves, David Crosby, Graham Nash, Stephen Stills, and Dallas Taylor at the house in Studio City. (HENRY DILTZ)

Dallas, 1969. (HENRY DILTZ)

BELOW: *(left to right)* Jerry Tolman, Dallas Taylor, Bonnie Bramlet, "Chocolate," Stephen Stills, Unknown, and Mike Finnigan. Drugs sabotaged Dallas' attempt to reunite with Stills and his band in 1978. (HENRY DILTZ)

David Crosby, 1970.
(GRAHAM NASH)

A pensive Graham Nash at Balboa
Stadium in San Diego, 1969.
(HENRY DILTZ)

Graham and Susan's birthday party, February, 1982. Seated around the
Trailways bus station chess game table are *(left to right)* Graham Nash,
Stephen Stills, and Gwen Roberts. Candy Finnegan stands behind Gwen.
(GRAHAM NASH)

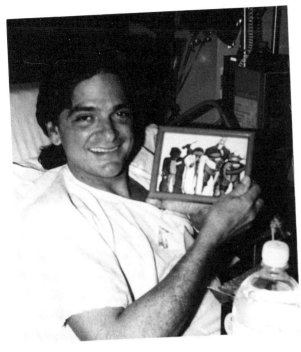

Dallas recovering from surgery—1 week after the liver transplant, 1990. (DALLAS TAYLOR)

Dallas and his wife Betty Wyman. (NEAL PRESTON)

Dallas and his grandson Stephen. (DALLAS TAYLOR)

Dallas' sister Darlene *(left)* and his
stepmother, Jeannie. (DALLAS TAYLOR)

Dallas' son Dallas and his daughter Sharlotte at the Transplant
Awareness Benefit given by Crosby, Stills, Nash, Young, Don Henley,
and the Desert Rose Band at the Santa Monica Civic Auditorium,
March 31, 1990 for financial assistance with Dallas' liver transplant.

(DALLAS TAYLOR)

Dallas and Betty. (NEAL PRESTON)

I'd risk being institutionalized for the rest of my life, so I resolved to deal with it alone. Some of these feared symptoms, however, could be checked out with the outside world and I did this as subtly as I could.

"Is it warm in here?" I asked timidly.

"Damned warm," Elaine said. "You'd think that for what we pay here, the least they could do is have decent air conditioning."

"Thank God!" I said under my breath. Now I had to figure out a way to find out if all the other guys had constant erections, too.

"Dallas," Lenny said, "where'd you go? Get your mind back here and get your hand away from that thing. Here. Finish making me some snowflakes and stop behaving like you're in a state mental hospital." Everyone was looking at me and smiling. I covered my groin with a pillow, took the snub-nosed scissors and construction paper, and tried to settle down.

"Looks like you could use a shower, Dallas," Jill said seductively. I didn't know how to take that. She either meant a cold one or was proposing a rendezvous. The showers were the area the staff watched the least and so were the best place to get your rocks off. I knew her meaning when she winked at me and I could hardly restrain myself from dragging her there that second. I was so turned on I could only tremble and sweat. This is not the kind of response women find attractive and she shuddered and quickly turned away.

"I know all about them showers, girl, so get it right out of your head," said Lenny, not taking his eyes from the TV. "Sex is a drug and there ain't no need to be fixing in my face."

"Well, for some of us it's been so long that you can hardly blame us," Elaine said. John smiled. Lenny waved her to be quiet. He was concentrating on the movie. He wanted Jimmy Stewart to believe Clarence so that Sheldon Leonard wouldn't throw them out of his saloon.

"*Believe*, Jimmy!" Lenny said, impersonating a gospel singer. "Believe that it can happen."

"I believe!" said Jill, clapping. "I believe!"

"You've got to believe, Jimmy! Believe, and anything can happen!" Lenny said.

"Do you believe, Dallas? Do you believe, Elaine? Do you believe, Jonathan?" Lenny asked loudly.

"I guess so," I whispered.

"Fuck you, queer," Elaine said.

"No," John said.

The fluorescent light from the hallway was suddenly eclipsed by an enormous toxic presence. I felt a rush of fear. All faces turned toward the door.

"What are you doing, Lenny?" bellowed an inhuman voice.

"Spending some quality time with my patients," he said, not taking his eyes from the TV. "Why don't you come on in here and join us?"

"Yeah, come on in, Mom," said Elaine. "We need someone to provide a strong male influence and Dad here ain't up to it."

The presence had scared me so much that I'd curled up as small as I could and was trying to hide in a corner of the couch. I was certain that this was the free-floating evil that I knew was lurking around, waiting for the first opportunity to come and get me. I had no idea what It was planning, but I knew that the end would be grisly. It would probably tear my flesh and rob my soul. Now Elaine and Lenny were talking with It, proof of their collaboration in the plot. I had to cope with a sense of enormous betrayal while at the same time trying to come up with an escape route.

"It's time for medications," It said, "line up outside the nurses' station."

"No! No! No!" I yelled and planted my face in the space between the arm and cushion of the couch.

"Dallas?" Lenny said. "It's just a damn multivitamin."

"More paranoid by the minute," the voice said. "I've got to tell Dr. Brett that you need a little vitamin H."

"Vitamin H" was what staff called Haldol and was what the detoxers who were crazy got. As I burrowed further, I could feel that a half-eaten piece of Christmas candy some- one had tucked into the couch was stuck on my eyebrow. As I tried to make myself even smaller, hoping to fade from their minds, I had the strong feeling that I'd done this before, years ago, when my parents were still together, and fighting. I felt two pairs of hands on me, carefully pulling me up. The hands on my shoulders were Lenny's, and they were cool and comforting.

"It's OK, Dallas," he said. "It's only a multivitamin. I'll take one, too." The other pair of hands just patted my back. They felt so bony and lethargic they had to be John's.

"Sit up and face it," Lenny said softly. "Sit up and face what's frightening you and we'll help you through it." Even though I was convinced that he was in collusion with the others, I slowly complied and pointed toward the door with- out looking at it.

"Nurse Ratchet is frightening you?" Lenny asked. "Well she frightens me, too, but she's not going to hurt you. Come on, sit up."

I sat up and turned and looked straight at her. Lenny was right. It was the floor nurse, whom we had dubbed Nurse

Ratchet, as a tribute to Ken Kesey and his *One Flew Over the Cuckoo's Nest*. While our nurse did have ratlike features, she was actually more indifferent than mean. She was a large-boned woman, covered in a puffy layer of fat that made it hard to see her eyes or her wedding ring. She always wore heavily starched white uniforms graced by different colored cardigans that reflected her mood. Today was green, which meant no danger. Because of the holiday she also wore a Santa Claus corsage. She smiled perfunctorily at me and her eyes disappeared along with most of my fear. She was something to dislike and avoid, but nothing to dread and I breathed a sigh of relief at my reprieve. Whatever it was that was out there, was still out there, but now I had more time to prepare for it.

"Bring the medication cart in here," Lenny said with his hand on my shoulder. "We'll all take our vitamins while watching Jimmy Stewart learn his lesson." Nurse Ratchet hesitated but finally acquiesced when Jill offered to help her.

"It's going to be better tomorrow," John said to me in a low whisper. "I've been through this many times. Everything is scary and possibly evil. No one can be trusted. This is how politicians and corporate vice presidents feel all the time. It will be better tomorrow and much better the day after." I wanted to say the same thing to him but I was still too shaky to talk. I was back to my pretend-everything-is-normal mode and didn't want them to have further evidence of my instability. I picked up the scissors and made an attempt to cut out a snowflake. Lenny sat down and disappeared back into his movie. John sat stiffly at the other end of the couch and disappeared back into his depression. Elaine eyed me eerily.

"What's going to hurt you, Dallas?" she said. I shrugged and kept on with my snowflake. The room was very warm and

I was either sweating an impossible amount or I'd wet my pants. I tried to think good thoughts: my wife coming to visit later in the afternoon, my upcoming session with Dr. Brett, seeing my kids, getting Jill into the shower, and the arrival of the cocaine that might restore my sanity. The last two made me feel best and so I stuck with them: sex and drugs, my two best friends.

"Come on, Dallas." Elaine pressed on. "What can hurt you? Are we talking slimy three-eyed demons from hell, or aliens sending you messages and reading your thoughts, or IRS agents or what?"

"What scares *you*?" John asked Elaine, to fend her off. "An eternity we've spent together and I still don't think I know the answer. It's not the obvious stuff: middle age, no money, losing your looks. I know those things don't truly bother you. What does?"

"Don't, John," she said, her teeth clenched. "You don't have the strength for this."

"I've never had the strength for anything, according to you, and that's never stopped you before. What scares you?"

"You learn the most important things about people when you learn that," Lenny said. "You want to understand somebody, don't ask them about their dreams; ask them about their nightmares. Look at Jimmy Stewart here."

"What scares you?" Elaine asked John. Her aggression was fading and she appeared to really want the answer.

"I know that I'm a failure by most standards. I don't have money or ambition, because I've always felt they were wrong. I've never been able to stay away from drugs and this I regret. The only thing that I have to be proud of is that I have tried to live a moral life. I've never tried to exploit or harm anyone. I may have failed with you and with our daughter, but I think those were errors of ignorance. The thing that scares me most is the possibility that, finally, it may not matter. Maybe no one is watching, no one cares, and that big karmic computer up in the sky that I've considered so important, is no more important than Lenny's Santa Claus. That terrifies me."

Elaine looked sad and Lenny dabbed at his eye with some of the tinsel from his corsage. Jimmy Stewart greeted the bank examiner and policeman waiting for him in his living room and ran upstairs looking for Donna Reed. I started feeling anxious again because here was something new to worry about.

"What scares me the most," Elaine said in a quavering voice, "is having no hope and being alone."

She should have gone to him then, comforted him, and allowed herself to be comforted, but instead she looked at the floor, thick tears dropping onto her pointed boot tips. John sat on the edge of our couch and appeared puzzled. I imagined that they were both thinking about the cocaine they'd arranged to smuggle in, and we all knew that, inevitably, it would lead to the realization of Elaine's fears. Hope would disappear with that first tingling sensation in the nostrils and John, who was circling the drain now and did not have another chance of recovery, would soon be gone, leaving Elaine alone. I imagined that they cared deeply for each other and that their partnership was more than their habit, convenience, and the "codependency" that Candy had been going on about. I also imagined that the only explanation for their paralysis was the combination of all of those things, which led to the painful conclusion that they should not be together. Together, they would both die. And now, unable to move forward or back away, they sat motionless.

I put down my pillow shield, got up from my wet cushion and stood between them. They had identified part of the thing that was outside waiting to devour me and in so doing removed a few of its teeth. I took Elaine's hand in one of mine and John's in the other and bridged their gap. The bell on Jimmy and Donna's Christmas tree started ringing. Lenny grabbed up the scissors and quickly fashioned a couple of orange snowflakes into a pair of wings which he scotch taped onto my back. Nurse Ratchet returned with the medication cart and stood in the door, smiling tolerantly. It reminded me of thousands of such smiles but instead of getting mad, instead of feeling bad and inferior, I aimed a smile at her that would melt steel. She patted her sweater, adjusted her cap, coughed, and silently turned away.

I skipped group and waited in the shower for forty minutes before Jill came. When it became apparent that she wasn't planning on coming on her own, I sent Paolo to find her and give her a note and a flower that I stole from an ugly bouquet that someone had left at the nurses' station for Nurse Ratchet. I'd already forgotten what I said in the note and so hoped that the lust of the moment would carry us over that part.

"What do you mean you think someone is trying to kill me?" she said angrily, both hands on her hips.

"I . . . meant it figuratively," I said, grasping her hand. She pulled it away. Her breasts, though small, were full and poked their eyes at me through her white cotton shirt. "I'm . . . worried about you."

"Why?" she said, ready to leave.

"Because . . . because I see you and Elaine headed on a collision course and I want to avoid it," I said. I was very happy with myself. I may well have been losing my mind but my instincts were all intact. She softened and sat down on the floor. I sat next to her and took her hand again and this time she didn't pull away. The tiles were very white and the grout was very brown. The floor felt cold on my butt.

"I can take care of myself, Dallas," she said. "If we collide, we collide. So what? What did you really want?"

"I know you're still vomiting," I said without thinking. "You're lying and it can kill you." I had no idea where that had come from. I hadn't been planning on mentioning it at all. Either my lust was in control, or I was actually concerned about her. My mouth was completely in charge of doing whatever the hell it wanted.

"Lenny told me what you did with Elaine and John," she said, playing with the wings that were still taped to my back. "You've never helped anyone but yourself in here. What's up?"

I covered my groin with my hand and wondered what my mouth would come up with next.

"They made me feel better because we have lots of the same fears. They made me feel less crazy and so I wanted to make them feel less alone," I said.

"That's not the Dallas I know," she said laughing. "Don't tell me you're sweet underneath?" I saw her flush and moisten. I quickly stood up.

"Why are you doing that? Where are you going?" she said.

"You're softening. My mind just clicked in and it was coming up with a hundred things to say to convince you that I am sweet and worth fucking — right here, right now. That's the only reason I got you down here. I think. Oh shit, I don't know anymore."

"You are full of surprises. Honesty — what's next? I know that's why you wanted me here; that's why I'm staying." She took my hand and pulled me down on top of her. She kissed me hard and had her shirt unbuttoned before I even realized what was happening.

"We have to move fast," she said, unzipping her jeans. I fumbled with my own pants and she had to help me. The tiles were hard and echoed every sound.

"Oh, my!" she said as I slipped off my underwear. "Mr. Happy is awfully glad to see me."

We joined immediately without even a pretense of fore-play, and she again said, "Oh, my!" at just the right moment, and in slightly less than that it was over.

"Damn it!" I said. "I'm sorry. It's never like this."

"It was perfect," she said. "Sweet. Like being a teenager again." She looked at her watch and started putting her shirt on. In my hurry I hadn't even touched her breasts. I did now, and she smiled.

"I'm feeling like a teenager all the time these days," I said. "I used to think I had control over my body. Now it's doing whatever the hell it wants."

"Well it seems that your Mr. Happy already wants to have another go at it," she said, giggling.

"Wow!" I said, realizing that she was right. "This is incredible! I'll probably start breaking out next."

"Ask Lenny if you can use the car," she said, inching down to a receptive position.

"First, gotta make up an excuse to tell Candy why I skipped group," I said getting on top of her.

"No need to do that," a voice behind us said. "Candy will find out the truth along with your doctor and the rest of the group. Now get up!"

Nurse Ratchet stood there, a medical chart in her hand and a flushed look of anxiety on her face. She was quivering with what I thought was righteous indignation but which Jill instantly recognized as sexual excitement.

"How long have you been there?" Jill asked her, not moving.

"Just long enough! Now get up and get out of here now!" she said.

"We're locked," I said. "Can't move. Like dogs." I laughed and lay on top of Jill.

"Unless you leave us alone for a few minutes we'll be stuck like this for the rest of our lives," Jill said

"You're right about being dogs," Nurse Ratchet said, "and you deserve to be treated like them." I heard the sound of a faucet being turned on and then water running. Within a second Jill and I were drenched. Jill started laughing and catching the water in her mouth and I did the same. Then Nurse Ratchet stormed out, giving us the perfect opportunity to finish, but "Mr. Happy" was embarrassed and didn't feel like staying out and playing anymore. We stood and did up our clothes and posed with soap in our hands until Ratchet returned with reinforcements. Lenny stood with his hands on his hips and a "tsk, tsk" on his lips as we pretended to be taking showers.

"You two are in a heap of trouble," he said, a smile on his face. "Maybe some reflection time will clean them dirty minds."

We sat in hard chairs in front of the nurses' station for an hour before Candy and the other counselors returned with the Christmas tree. We weren't allowed to change our clothes or talk to each other or smoke or move until our fate was determined by the group. I felt good about what happened because I had been honest and was only half responsible for breaking the rules. I felt terrifically close to Jill and held her hand whenever Lenny and Ratchet were out of sight: I thought that I might want to spend the rest of my life with her and decided to be honest with my wife later and tell her about it. Being with Elaine and John that morning had convinced me that my wife would be better off without me, and anyway, I was sure that she already had someone else. She'd gone to the Warner Bros. Christmas party the night before and hadn't gone home. I knew this because I'd telephoned the house every fifteen minutes all night long and there'd been no answer. Between calls, I lay in bed sweating and waiting for something bad to happen, and I made a mental list of all the people she was probably sleeping with, and another of all the people in my life who'd betrayed me. At the top of each list was Stills, and I kept seeing her in his arms in my bed.

This image of Stephen was common, even comforting, because I'd made him the source of all my problems for at least a decade. He had not protected me in CSN and he had fired me from Manassas. He had knocked up Laura, my second wife, and spread it around town that my arms were "shot" because I was a junkie. He had even, I heard, told Paul McCartney not to hire me when he was looking for a drummer for Wings because I was unreliable. And when you get down to it, Stills was the reason I'd gotten all fucked up in the first place. After CSN&Y had broken up for good I starting spending a lot of time with him and we were doing more coke than ever and drinking more booze than ever to even out the coke jag. I really didn't like booze, but the more coke I did, the more I drank. One day I mentioned this to a roadie. "Man," I said, "I wish there was some other way to come down. Quaaludes make me stupid and pot makes me paranoid and sleepers give me too much of a hangover." The roadie grinned and laid out two white lines of powder. "Here, man, try this," he said. I thought, "Right! Just what I need, more coke," but I snorted it anyway. Then, something happened—my jaw went slack and my body relaxed and I felt *well*. I looked at the roadie quizzically and he said, "It's smack; china white." I guess I still looked puzzled because he added, "You know, heroin, man." "Oh, yeah, of course," I said, trying to sound like I'd known all along. What I did know, though, was that this was the medicine I'd been looking for. Not long after, it was the only medicine I needed.

"*Fuck!* I can't find a vein!" I said, trying to jab the needle into my arm. My blood was trickling down and I thought I could hear it splatter as it hit my boot. "Let me help," a voice said and I looked over at him and remembered that I was locked in a bathroom with Keith Richards. Even a few months earlier I would have been impressed to no end but now all that mattered was finding a working vein so I could get well. Keith grabbed my arm, and squeezed it at the biceps and finally, the blood filled the syringe. The heroin solution was boiling hot because it had just been cooked, but that didn't matter and I plunged it in hard and fast. My nose instantly stopped running and I felt like having a conversation.

"So what's happening with the Stones, Keith?" I slurred.

"Fucking Mick's a wanker," he said while preparing his hit.

"Is it true you and Mick fucked Mick Taylor in the ass?" He didn't answer. I watched him slide the needle into his arm. "I thought I heard that somewhere. . . . Well, that's one way to get a gig."

I was having trouble getting gigs, and I was broke. I was staying wherever I could—for a while I even lived at the

Record Plant in Sausalito. The owners of the studio, Chris Stone, the businessman partner, and Gary Kelgrin, the wild creative-genius partner, knew me from various dates. Bill Wyman did his solo albums there, which I had worked on, and they put me up. Gary and I became friendly, and he was one of the few people who easily outdistanced me in "getting high." When Gary drowned in his pool a few of his friends called it murder, but most of us assumed that Gary had gone into the water so high that he'd literally forgotten how to swim.

The Record Plant was designed by some deranged architect to be the ultimate in decadence, and it reflected Gary's life and death exactly. Built to cater to the needs and whims of the rock stars who would spend days at a time holed up in the studio working on their albums, it was perfect for multiple orgies and general mayhem. It featured a jacuzzi and several "theme" bedrooms: the Rock Room was actually the S and M room; there was a psychedelic room; and the Sissy Room was all done up in frilly pastels and lace. No matter how desperate I got, I could never bring myself to stay there. When I had a choice, I'd stay in the Boat Room, which was built to resemble a sailboat, portholes and all.

After a while, the kindness of friends and strangers was wearing real thin. I should have been a rich man and not had any of these problems, but I got screwed out of it all. I was completely strung out when I called Stephen for the what was probably the millionth time. We had gotten together recently to play, to try to recapture some of the magic, but it didn't work and Stephen got pissed. "This is it," he said, "you've lost it." But soon after that session, I really needed help, so I called him up. I didn't catch him at a good time, and he answered the phone with an irritated, "What!"

"Hey, Stephen, it's Dallas. Look, man, I'm really sick and I'm broke."

"Dallas — *no!*" he said. "You'll just put it up your arm."

"I promise you, I'll quit, I want to quit, I'm just too sick now to think. I need time to think." There was a long silence.

Then I played my ace, "Stephen, I'll drop the lawsuit if you'll just give me ten grand."

Stephen and I had begun collaborating in 1971 in what would become Manassas, joined this time by ex-Byrd Chris Hillman. The three of us had coproduced the band's two albums. I was now suing Stephen because I hadn't received any royalties for the albums, although I was promised ten percent. Just as in CSN, our contract was a verbal agreement and the deal was sealed with a handshake and a hug — after all, we were a family. "No contracts," he'd said. "We don't need a piece of paper to come between us — our word is our bond." But he'd "forgotten" to pay me, so I sued.

"OK, Dallas, you got a deal. Sign away all rights to all the stuff — CSN, my solo stuff, everything — and I'll write you that check for ten thousand dollars. I'll have my lawyers draw up the papers tomorrow."

"Tomorrow!! Jesus, man, I can't fucking wait till tomorrow! I'm sick, I need dope, I can't fucking wait that long."

"I'll see you tomorrow," he said, and hung up. Oh, God, how the hell did I get here? How the hell was I going to get through the next twenty-four hours?

My hand was shaking as I signed on the dotted line. My lawyer, Stan Diamond, was angry and thoroughly disgusted with me. "Don't do it, Dallas. You're signing away a fortune." But I didn't care, I just wanted it to be over with, I just wanted to get well. Then Stan handed me a check for six thousand dollars.

"What the fuck is this?" I yelled.

"That's your money," he said. "I took my forty percent of the ten grand and that's what's left."

The City National Bank was just across the street but it seemed miles away as I stumbled and ran across Wilshire Boulevard.

"Do you have any I.D.?" the teller asked while she stared at my check.

My heart was pounding and I was sweating. I knew I smelled bad; junkies do when they need a fix. "No," I replied, "but if you'll just call Mr. Diamond, he'll tell you it's me."

She gave me a look of disgust and contempt—like only a bank teller can—and went to consult with one of the other tellers. They both looked at me as if I were about to rob the place and then my teller picked up the phone and made a call. When she came back, I was practically gasping.

"How would you like this, sir?" she asked.

"Hundreds," I said. She counted out sixty one-hundred dollar bills. I grabbed them up, crammed them in my pocket and ran for the dealer.

The money lasted five days.

So when you come down to it, I thought, Stills was the source of all my problems, and now he had my wife, too. At least my demon had a face.

My demon had a face, that is, until last night. Then, lying there it occurred to me that I was there because of my own actions. Stephen Stills had done nothing that I hadn't done or was capable of doing. He hadn't made me a junkie; he was not the reason my life had not worked. He had, in fact, been my closest friend for a good part of my life. He had given me as many jobs as he had taken away. He saved me from myself countless times and clearly didn't deserve the rap I had given him in order to avoid taking it myself. When I realized this, the image of Stephen in my wife's arms faded from its place in my mind, and I was relieved to realize that the years of drugs and chemicals had not irrevocably taken from me the ability to reason. But at the same time, I felt so overwhelmed with anxiety that I had to get up and turn on the light over the bed. The evil thing that had been after me no longer had a face, so it could be *anybody*, including myself.

"What do you think they'll do to us?" Jill whispered.

"Writing assignment. Restriction from each other," I said. "You look pretty when you're wet."

She smiled and put her head down until a tech passed by. I wanted to tell her I loved her, but after my amateurish performance, I didn't want to further convince her that I had the emotional maturity of a fourteen year old.

"Candy will yell a lot. I may have to get into a fight with her," she said. "What's it like to be famous?"

The question surprised me. I'd been here for almost two weeks and no one ever alluded to my former life. Either they thought it should be avoided until I was better equipped for the tough stuff, or they'd never heard of the bands I'd played with and didn't care.

"I don't really remember," I said. "I think it was easy."

"Easy?" she asked. "People *watching* you all the time. What do you mean, 'easy'?"

I was trying to formulate a response when John walked up and waved for us to follow him.

"It's time to decorate the tree," he said. "Candy told me to come and get you." As we stood, we looked at each other and shrugged. Undoubtedly she was planning on dismembering us in front of everybody rather than in private. We followed him to the TV room and stood in the door, waiting.

"Come on in!" Candy said cheerfully. "Lenny, put on that Christmas music of yours."

She stood in front of an unnaturally green pine tree that a tech was trying to balance and tie. Elaine sat smoking a cigarette and looking at her watch; the cocaine was due any minute. John walked all around the room looking at the tree from every possible angle and was obviously happy with what he saw.

"It looks just like a real one but we will all rest comfortably tonight knowing that nothing died for our fun."

"I know I will," Elaine said.

"Hey man, it's like *The Brady Bunch*," Paolo said examining the paper chains and snowflakes that Lenny had been making all day. Lenny put on his Supremes Christmas album and started dancing. The music sounded tinny and scratched. Jill and I stood by the door unable to move.

"Come in," Candy said. "We took a vote and decided we want you with us to decorate the tree. We've also decided on twenty-four hour reflection time and restriction from each other. No talking or touching each other until we say you can. Got it?" She turned toward the tree and we nodded to her back. I felt cheated.

"Is that all?" I asked her.

"I don't think your behavior deserves any more attention, Dallas. Do you?" she said, not looking at me.

"Yes!" I said. "I need to be . . . straightened out! Yelled at!

"Elaine, would you yell at Dallas for me?" Candy said, reaching for a box of decorations.

"Be happy to," Elaine said. "How far do you want me to go?"

"As far as I would," Candy said, looking for the perfect place to put a strand of chains cut from the pages of *People* magazine.

"Put that right in the center," Lenny directed her, "so that we can see Tom Selleck sitting by that palm tree."

Elaine put a chair in the middle of the room and then led me to it. She cracked her knuckles, flexed her deltoids, and stretched her calves. She put her hands on the arm rests on either side of me and put her face directly in front of mine, making sure that I was pinned and that my personal space was thoroughly violated. She looked meanly in my eyes, then turned her face to the side and spit her gum across the room in the general direction of the wastebasket.

"Go ahead," she said, her lips almost touching my nose. "Go ahead and give us the excuse. Tell us why you lied to our faces and spit on the program. Go ahead."

Even though it was not what I wanted, it was better than feeling that I had gotten away with something because the other patients liked or pitied me. I closed my eyes and imagined that it was Candy and not Elaine and let my mouth do whatever it wanted.

"I didn't lie. I was completely up front with Jill. What happened was honest and good. This one rule is stupid," I said.

"What other rules do you discard as stupid?" Elaine said. Candy turned around and smiled. "Do you throw away every rule that gets in your way?"

"No," I said, "but this sex that we had was . . . pure. It was good and natural. It wasn't a fix or anything like that. I think I may love Jill," I said regretting the words even as they left my lips.

"That is pitiful," Elaine said. "You are so fucking confused and crazy that you walk around here thinking that something is trying to kill you, you even pee in your pants because you think old Ratchet is going to give you some Haldol, and yet this same mind picks and chooses the rules it wants to follow because it knows which ones are good and which ones are stupid. That doesn't sound smart to me. Does it to you, Dallas?" she said. Her mouth was inches from my eyes, as if she calculated this as my most vulnerable location. When I opened them all I could see were her cracked lips and gapped teeth. From the silence around me, I could tell that everyone had stopped to listen. Someone had taken the needle off Diana Ross and I could hear only Elaine's breathing.

"Not when you put it like that," I said.

"Your fucked-up demented, pathetic excuse for a mind is what got you in here and what is going to get your sorry ass kicked out unless you start listening to someone who knows something. These rules exist because they work, and you're going to follow them or I'm going to rip you a new asshole," she said. Someone laughed and she turned on them. I stole a look at her face. It was hard and foaming and I realized that there was a very good chance that she would bite me. When she turned back to me, I nodded, hoping to save my nose.

"What's this nodding shit?" she asked. "Use that golden rock star voice of yours. Did you hear what I said?"

"Yes," I said, suddenly grateful that this was Elaine and not Candy. Candy would have held back when she sensed an old wound opening. Elaine went for the kill. I didn't want anybody to hold back anymore. I wanted it all.

"I never had a good voice. I sang backup but never lead," I said.

"Of course not. You need talent and conviction to do that. The only talent you have left is for whining and getting people to pity you so much they'll throw you a charity fuck. Tell me, do you really even know how to play drums? Sorry, stupid question. What's to know? You hit something with a stick. I'm sure even you can handle that. But then, why did you get fired? Tell me, Jill, is he any good with his stick?" Jill smiled and looked at the floor.

"I'll bet you're incompetent at that, too," she said. "Tell me, Dallas, what are you good at, other than dragging down the people you claim to love?"

"He didn't drag me down, bitch," Jill said. "I go only where I want."

"Ah, the vomit princess comes even further out of her shell. *You* are another story. You must think a lot of yourself to fuck a paranoid junkie on the same floor that you puke on every day. We all know it. You haven't been fooling anyone," Elaine said. Jill shot up, arms outstretched, ready to hit Elaine but Lenny grabbed Jill and eased her back into her chair.

"Did you see that, Dallas? She was going to defend you. Why are women always doing that for you? Where's your backbone?" Elaine said.

"Under your foot," I said, "ready to be snapped. Do it."

"That's enough!" Candy said. She came over and pried Elaine's hands from the chair.

"Another woman to the rescue, Dallas," Elaine said. "You're never going to learn to walk if mommy is always there to prevent you from falling."

"That's enough, Elaine. Put something on the tree. Lenny, give her a snowflake to put on the tree," Candy said.

Lenny handed her a purple one and she crumpled it into a ball and threw it at the tree. She returned to her seat, lit a fresh cigarette and glowed with malevolence.

"You don't have to take care of me," I said, standing. "I can do it myself."

"Not yet," Candy said. "You've been asleep for over twenty years, Dallas. You're a scared teenager just waking up. You got everything to learn."

"Why'd you do that?" Jill asked Candy angrily. "Why'd you let her do your job?"

"Pay attention," John said. "She's doing her job. She's got them both right where they should be and she's not being the heavy or rewarding the two of them with attention. This woman is an artist."

"I'm expecting a visitor," Elaine said abruptly standing and knocking over her chair. Lenny put the Supremes back on midsong.

"This ain't *The Brady Bunch*," Paolo said, back at the tree with some tinsel. "Looks like white folks have the same Christmases as we do, only no one's got a broken nose yet."

"Are you sure you want to see this visitor?" John asked, as Elaine reached the door. "Maybe we should stay here and decorate the tree together."

Elaine paused and turned back toward him. He held out his thin hand for what seemed a very long time and she looked at it closely, avoiding his face altogether. Something she saw in that hand helped her make her decision, and I looked to see what it was as she resolutely walked out of the room. The hand was the same dirty, yellow, clawless crab that I'd always seen with one difference: there was a tremor now. With Elaine's fear of being alone it made sense that she would reject something that was going to die soon, but her resolve was remarkably unlike anything that I felt I'd ever be able to muster. Elaine was gone. I wondered what would happen to her daughter and to John and I wondered who would be the next one to leave.

The likelihood of early departures was great, and the potential for pain enormous. I smiled at Jill, filled with hope for our new love, and sat back down, gripping the chair to steady myself. I was starting to tremble — cocaine was close by and easily had. The impulse to run after Elaine and lose everything was so overpowering that it terrified me.

"Telegrams, long distance telephone calls, and visitors. Never trust them, my mother used to say. They always bring bad news," John said.

"You can stop her," Jill said. "That's what all that stuff about having a backbone was about. She wants you to stop her."

"No, I can't," he said. "It's years past that. She's gone." Candy looked at John and then Jill and then me trying to read our faces. She ran from the room, waving at Lenny to follow.

"Isn't it a pretty tree?" John said, reaching for the box of tinsel. "We had a real one that we kept alive in a bucket out back that we used every year for almost ten years. Went to get it one Christmas Eve and someone had cut it down. The bucket couldn't have weighed more than ten, twenty pounds but rather than take the whole thing they preferred to kill it. It was like losing a member of the family. Never bothered to get another. This is the first time I've ever been able to stomach a plastic tree, I suppose that's growth. Come on, Dallas, let's help each other overdecorate this damned tree." He reached over and helped me up from my chair. "The doomed leading the blind. You'll have to write a song about this."

Candy chased Elaine for three blocks before falling over a fire plug and spraining her ankle. She came back limping and mad at herself for not being faster or more cunning. She blamed herself for every AWOL, and for the next two days she held marathon groups that focused primarily on what she had done.

"You're taking this too personally," John said, his crossed legs holding his bladder shut. "Elaine has eloped from every major detox center in Southern California. There is no stopping her. It's not your fault." It was the second day, Christmas day, and we'd been sitting in group for five hours without cigarettes or bathroom breaks.

"This is very personal," Candy said, looking at the ankle she was resting on a chair. It was swollen and red like her eyes; she was wearing the same clothes she had worn yesterday. She looked and smelled like a new admission and was every bit as unpredictable. "I'm responsible for you. Elaine could be dead by now. You can fuck up, you're drug addicts in a hospital, you're supposed to. I can't. What didn't I do with her and what haven't I done with all of you so that you wouldn't tell me what she was planning?"

"Can we please have a cigarette?" Jill said, near tears. She was taking this as hard as Candy and she also looked unwashed and overtired.

"Why is this bothering you so much?" Paolo asked Jill. "You hated this chick. You two were always going at each other."

"Do you feel guilty, Jill?" I asked. "We all knew about it. We were all going to do some. We're all guilty."

"I just want a damn cigarette!" she said, jumping up and walking to the window.

"Back in the chair," Candy said forcefully. The room was too bright and too warm. The plastic Christmas tree was only half decorated and it leaned to one side. Half naked and drooping, it was a perfect symbol for the group and for the moment. Jill sat back down, pulled her knees up to her chin and started crying.

"People always leaving or dying," said Paolo. "Best just to let it go and not get close."

"That's what I'm afraid of," Candy said. "Maybe I've been at this too long. Maybe I didn't believe that Elaine could really make it and so I didn't give it my all."

"I have seen hundreds of counselors and therapists and family and friends and cops and quick-stop market cashiers and strangers give Elaine their all, and it never makes any difference," John said, wincing in pain. "As for us, well, I guess I should say, as for me, I think you've gone out of your way to make this happen for me, and I think it *is*. I have no plans of going anywhere and at the moment have no thoughts of smuggling anything in. I am, however, giving some serious thought to peeing in my pants if you don't let me go the restroom very soon." Candy smiled slightly but quickly shrugged off the compliment and sunk back into her doubt.

"You didn't think I was going to stay," I said. "Nobody did. And yet you got close to me. Well, I feel close to you, anyway. Shit! You've been standing behind me every god-damned second! I've walked out of a shitload of places just like this and I'm still here only because of you. Straight out. You're the only recovering person I've ever met who's sleazier than I am." She turned her face toward me and gave me a direct smile. There were tears in her eyes that glistened in the fluorescent lighting and I had a déjà vu that was gone as soon as it appeared. The hair, raspy voice, slight southern twang, street toughness, tattoos, bracelets, braless boobs, and tears reminded me of someone but no name came. The tears were the key; I'd had the same feeling the other time I'd seen her really cry.

138

"A burned-out old broad like me ain't going to be fooled by no sweet-talking southern boy," she said. "This is my fault. I'm sorry I let you all down." Jill cried louder and Paolo looked tensely at the nicotine stains on his hands.

"I was planning on leaving tonight," he said, not looking at anyone. "I called my homeboys this morning. They'll be here at dinner." Candy turned toward him and smiled only at the corners of her eyes. My mouth dropped when I realized what she was doing. Blaming us for Elaine's AWOL would have been met with anger, lies, and excuses and would have left us demoralized. Blaming herself, on the other hand, had just the opposite effect. All along she had been using her candor and vulnerability to fish for something—and she had just hooked a big one.

"Why, Paolo?" Candy asked.

"I ain't like these people," he said. "I ain't got a job, or education—I don't even know anyone who does. All I got is my homeboys, and when I leave here, I'm going right back to the same life. Everybody uses back there, man. There ain't no way I can hang with sober people."

"You can change that if you want to," Candy said, gaining momentum. "I was a junkie biker chick. You think it was easy for me? I didn't finish ninth grade, never had a job, never fucking got up before noon unless I'd been too wired to make it to bed at all. Lying, cheating, whoring, and getting fucked up was all I knew, and I was good at it! Damned good at it! I wasn't exactly prepared for the job world three years ago when I got clean! I had to leave my old man, who was crazy and possessive *and* my dealer. I had to say goodbye to all of my friends that were still alive, do six months in jail for an old possession rap, and beg some chick I'd only known for two weeks to let me move in with her. Do you know what she did? She laughed in my face! And so did the next one! Then, after three weeks of sleeping in a car that belonged to someone in the program's, I found someone who was willing to take a chance on me. I got a job cleaning houses, got my own apartment, met people at meetings, and got this job, new friends, a new old man, and here I am. I am the fucking American Dream, Paolo. If I can do it, anyone can."

"Maybe you're stronger than me," Paolo said. "I ain't nothing without my people."

"Exactly wrong!" Candy said. "You ain't nothing with them! Man, with them, you go nowhere. You stay fucked up all the time! Feel bad all the time! In here, you've been yourself. A good, strong, warm, and honest man. Believe me, Paolo, you're all you've got. How many of your homeboys been in to visit you?"

"They don't like hospitals," Paolo answered defensively.

"I've never met anyone who does, my man," she said. "Face it. You're in a hole and you're the only one who can pull you out of it. You're all you've got, Paolo. I'm all I've got. No one is going to take care of me. I've got to do it by myself."

"When you first came in here, you didn't even know your own name," John said. "Look how far you've already come. Don't leave. I really like you."

"I need a roommate who doesn't mind my screaming, pacing and sleeping with the lights on," I said.

"You're so young," Jill said dully, to her knees. "You can't see it now, but the whole world is out there for you. Just hang on." She sounded as if she were repeating a phrase she'd heard a thousand times, and wished that it held some meaning for her. All eyes were on Paolo, who just sat there without expression.

"You told us, Paolo, so you must have wanted us to talk you out of it. Listen to that part of you that told us," Candy said. He smiled and slowly nodded. Candy hobbled over to hug him and she held him for a very long time. Even though I felt she had just reeled Paolo in like a marlin and was now finalizing the catch with a stranglehold that would not allow him to wriggle and flop off the boat, I had to believe that her concern and affection were genuine. She signaled that group was over for now and she had everyone give everyone supportive hugs. Then John ran off for the bathroom, Paolo ran to the phone to cancel his breakout and Lenny raced in dressed as Santa Claus, wearing a black beard and a tastefully tailored, hiphugging, violet Santa suit and carrying a big pillowcase filled with brightly wrapped presents and more decorations. Jill moved to a corner of the room and sat by herself. Candy watched her and then turned to see where I'd gone. She whispered something to Lenny and then went over and sat next to Jill.

I lit a cigarette and felt guilty about what I hadn't said. Paolo had confessed his AWOL plans and I had swallowed mine. In my morning session with Dr. Brett I had told him about what I had gone through a few nights ago and he had told me that it meant that my paranoia was diminishing and would soon be gone, but I thought that he didn't know what he was talking about—I knew this was not the case. A faceless demon was chasing me; a terrible insomnia was plaguing me; I was having revenge fantasies that were so real they had to be hallucinations; it was perfectly obvious that I was insane and the only way that I knew I could be held together was by drugs. Without them, my madness would progress to the point where I would end up in a Haldol stupor, institutionalized in some state hospital. Craziness, depression, and self-destructiveness had been in my family for generations, and I wanted to avoid my destiny at all costs. Drugs for medicinal purposes – if I came up with the right prescription, it could work. A little speed for the depression; a little pot for my nerves; if the speed didn't work then maybe a little coke, but not much and never a needle. No methadone. That junk had gotten me in here in the first place. And no booze. My uncles had died of it and just a week ago, an internist here had told me that I had the beginnings of cirrhosis.

"Let's all get in here and finish this damn Christmas tree or Santa ain't going to be giving out no presents this year," said Lenny to no one. Candy and Jill were continuing their conversation and I was continuing with my cigarette and a revenge fantasy which came from nowhere. It was remarkably vivid, and it involved Graham Nash and a chainsaw.

"You watching a TV in your head, boy?" Lenny asked me. "Get your sick ass up here and decorate this damn tree." He pulled from his pillowcase a long set of tiny lights and handed me an end to untangle.

"Had to bring this from my house," he said. "They were all out at the drugstore. Only had the kind that stay on all the time and that wouldn't do. Hospitals need blinking lights. Gotta keep the drug addicts' attention. Hello, Dallas?" I was watching Candy and Jill on the couch. Jill had stopped crying and was shaking her head and finger angrily.

"Dallas? Are you there?" Lenny said. He snapped the light strand taut and pulled me over to him. "Boy, you got the attention span of a three year old. I want you to talk to me. Keep talking until I tell you to shut up. Do you hear me?"

"Of course I hear you," I said. "I was just . . . distracted."

"That's why you're going to talk to me. Start moving them lips."

"What do you want me to talk about? What I'm thinking?" I asked.

"Not unless it's interesting. Save the dull shit for Dr. Brett and tell me all the good stuff. All the crazy, depraved shit that you're afraid to tell anyone."

"Why?" I asked.

"Help you with your attention span, help us get the damn tree done, and help me take my mind off my own crazy, depraved shit," he said. He finished unravelling the lights and pulled a chair over to stand on.

"I keep having all these thoughts of revenge: I don't plan them or anything. They just pop into my head. No controlling them or anything. Like now."

"So what's going on now?" he asked.

"I'm holding David Geffen's head underwater," I said.

"Why? What did he do to you?" he said, shoving a white light up the dress of the angel that was to go on the top of the tree.

"Nothing. Nothing at all. He ignored me. Never looked me in the eyes. Spoke about me as if I was in another room or too fucked up or stupid to understand things. He looks a lot better blue. WOW!"

"What's happening now?"

"Shark. Ripped his heart out. It was pretty small. About the size of a cashew."

"Sounds like my supervisor. Can you believe the bitch made me come in on Christmas? This boy has got better things to do than spend his favorite holiday with a bunch of burned-out honkies who don't even notice the fucking Christmas tree or give a sweet damn about all the trouble he went to cheer their sorry lives up. Give me that box of tinsel."

"I like the tree. I like your Santa suit. Thanks," I said.

"I don't need your damn sympathy," he said. "Just keep talking about what's in your head. Keep me company, for a change."

"OK. Chainsaw. I'm in my neighborhood, Silverlake, looking for someone. It's night. It's an electric chainsaw with an orange cord that's a mile long. Whoa! There's Graham's house. Whoa! Here he comes running down the stairs trying to run into my saw. He keeps lunging for the blade and I keep pushing him away."

"Why? Let it rip!" he said.

"He makes me feel too guilty. Manipulates me into believing that he's innocent and a good guy."

"Honey, you don't need to hear that noise. Cut off his head," he said.

"Ha! Can't catch him! He grew another pair of legs and is dodging and weaving like a rat in a maze. I knew that was in him."

"Put a chainsaw in a man's face and you see his true colors. OK. Switch the channel," he said.

"A needle. A big, fucking needle. Big as a redwood. Gleaming, blue metal. People being impaled on it like pieces of paper. Sliding down from the point, all the way to the bottom, and stacking up on top of each other. My first wife, my second wife, Ahmet Ertegun, my landlord. Wow! Here comes Joan Baez. Wriggling and shrieking like she was watching baby seals getting clubbed or something."

"Why is Joan Baez there?" he asked, putting tinsel on a branch, strand by strand.

"She's a bitch. Stuck up. Needs a good fuck," I said.

"Well, who doesn't?" he said, giggling. He stood away from the tree to find the next spot that needed tinsel. "Now,

---

144

don't you take that as encouragement. I ain't encouraging anything. You keep your hands off Jill. A hospital ain't no place for poking."

John came back in, looking very relieved, and he joined us at the tree. Lenny handed him a box of white styrofoam snowballs and a handful of paper clips.

"Bend the clips out and jam them into the balls," Lenny said. John seemed to have trouble focusing through his smudged and greasy glasses, and Lenny grabbed them and started wiping them with the pillowcase.

"These things been driving me crazy for a week now. Why the hell don't you clean them yourself?" Lenny said.

"Then I won't have anything to blame for not seeing things that I should see," John said.

"Well get your damn eyes checked and change your prescription, but don't keep grossing us all out," Lenny said, handing them back to him.

"I meant that figuratively," John said.

"Right," said Lenny picking up more tinsel. "Put the damn snowballs on the damn tree."

"Not in the best of moods today, are we?" John asked.

"His supervisor made him come in and no one here appreciates him," I said.

"Untrue," John said. "I happen to know that Lenny has today off. You came in here today because you wanted to."

"How the hell do you know that?" Lenny asked. He had his hands on his hips and was acting annoyed.

"I see lots of things that I shouldn't. Like nursing schedules cut into paper chains."

"You volunteered to come in today?" I asked.

"Who the hell else is going to bring you joy and peace in this damn place? Put the damn snowballs on the tree and,

Dallas, get back to the matinee in your head," Lenny said. The tree was even more dangerously tilted under the weight of these new decorations and Lenny moved to stabilize it by tying it down with more string.

"Don't!" John said. "It's perfect! It's just like all of us. How much can you put on a person before he falls over?" Lenny made a face and ran the string from the tree and to a couch leg. Suddenly the conversation between Jill and Candy got very loud and Jill ran from the room. Candy stood slowly and hobbled after her. Lenny noticed my impulse to follow them.

"That's their business," he said. "Keeping me entertained is yours."

"A scalpel," I said. "A razor-sharp scalpel and a pair of tweezers. I'm performing an autopsy on someone still alive. Lots of screaming and spraying blood; so much blood on the floor my shoes are sticking to it. I remove the intestines first. They're all tangled up."

"Who is it? Who is it?" Lenny asked, excited.

"I can't see. Too much blood. Someone . . . brown and wearing . . . a violet suit. Tied up by a strand of electric lights."

"That's not funny. You think that's funny?" Lenny said. "Go find me some damn extension cords."

I walked slowly from the room and once out of sight, ran down the hall looking for Jill. I searched all the patient bedrooms and slowed down only when passing the nursing station. Nurse Ratchet was yelling at someone from maintenance and Candy was on the telephone. I turned back and saw Jill coming out of the bathroom. She looked up and saw me motioning her to stay still. I eased myself past the nurses and caught up with Jill. I took her by the arm and we walked to the end of the hall. We pushed open the door to the unit and stood by the elevators. We were off the unit and well out of sight.

"We shouldn't be out here," she said, clearly still upset.

"What's wrong?" I asked. "You've got to tell me."

"Everything. Nothing. I feel bad about Elaine. I feel like I might be next. I feel bad that I'm still making myself puke and worse that I'm spending Christmas in here. That's all."

"What about us? Do you feel good about that?" I asked. "I'm going to tell my wife when she comes in. She won't mind. She's got somebody lined up. It's you and me from here on in." She laughed and hugged me just as the elevator arrived, letting off a janitor. I held open the elevator door and pulled her in.

"Where are we going?" she asked, scared and excited.

"Here. Just here," I said, pushing several buttons to get the elevator to pause between floors. I took her hand and kissed it and then her lips, and then I started ripping off my clothes as fast as I could. She kissed me back and did the same, and within a minute we were together again. We made love like grown-ups this time, slow and experienced, and when we were almost done, the elevator started to move. It ascended half a floor before we could get disentangled and when the door opened, in walked Candy. Her face was white with rage and her hands were clenched in purple fists and she exploded with a fury that I had only imagined could exist. She dragged both of us, undressed, our clothes in our arms, back onto the unit. She continued with the barrage while we got dressed and then made the entire group go back to the TV lounge for another marathon session. Lenny gave me hate stares for ruining his tree trimming, singing, and gift giving, and John ran to empty his bladder again before we started.

147

We sat there until midnight dealing with our inability to deal with anything and then we were allowed to go to bed for five hours to rest up for another day of the same. When we woke, Jill was gone. She'd left through a window, leaving everything she owned and a note on her bed for me. The note said only: "Dallas, this is not your fault." Candy disagreed with this and for the next few days I had another reason to plan my own escape: Jill needed someone to take care of her.

7

The Prison

I wake up at ten minutes to the hour, every hour, because the pain medication they give me every sixty minutes lasts only fifty. The pain is manageable now, but I know it will get worse and will become uncontrollable if I let anxiety in, so I try not to fight the restraints on my arms or the respirator breathing for me. Anxiety produces adrenaline, speeding up every system and organ, and I do not want my new liver overworked too soon. If my body rejects this liver then there will be nothing for them to do but open me back up and pray that another one becomes miraculously available. This happens to very few people but I am convinced that I will be one of them. It took six months to find this liver and I have already used up my fair share of miracles in this life.

Betty is sitting on the bed, smiling warmly and looking tired. She is almost too cheerful, talking on about how well everything is going and how close they are to removing the respirator. I try to see her eyes for the full story, but I can't focus well enough yet. Then Betty removes a stack of get well cards from her purse. I have been working in a hospital as a substance abuse counselor for three years now and have been involved in the lives of thousands of kids. There are many cards.

She selects a few and reads them, speaking loudly and quickly, because she knows she is competing with the pain for my attention. My gaze is directed behind her head, at the clock on the wall which I can't help staring at for ten minutes of each hour. It has become an enemy.

Betty is reading a card from a fourteen year old, an orphaned, violent skinhead who wanted to be a drummer. There is another card from a seventeen-year-old gang-banger who expected to and wanted to die before he was twenty. She reads the words of a thirteen-year-old girl, a model who sliced her wrists every time she was molested and came to us nearly autistic, forearms covered in tracks. All kids who affected us deeply — all successes. All of them working on their internal scars rather than running from them and still young enough to avoid ending up here, like me.

Betty sees my eyes on the clock and senses my drifting away from her. She sits closer and massages my shoulder. Her hands and eyes are strong and confident. Four years ago she picked me out of a crowd of nervous, nearly drowning new hospital aides. She gave support and encouragement and then, love, to a thirty-nine-year-old man who had never before held down a regular job and had no idea what a time clock was, let alone how to use it. Two years later she said she would marry me, and against the advice of nearly all her friends and family, and in front of a crowd of some of the most powerful people in Los Angeles, under a tent in the backyard of her mother's Bel Air mansion, she unwaveringly repeated the promise. Pretty, rich, well-bred, and educated, she became the partner of an ex-junkie, a thrice-divorced, has-been musician with a police record, no high school diploma, and one grandchild.

Six months ago, we didn't have a name for what was wrong with me, but we knew that I was getting sicker and sicker, and we were dreading the worst. On the night I was admitted to Cedars Sinai Hospital for internal bleeding she held my hand, running alongside the wheelchair driver as he rushed me from Emergency to a private room. Halfway down the corridor she came to an abrupt stop, almost turning the chair over. On the wall was a bronze plaque which she read once, then twice. Then she ran down the hall ahead of us.

While the nurses and business people got their fluid samples and their forms signed, Betty sat quietly on the other side of the room, wrapped in her heavy leather jacket. Twenty minutes later, we were alone in the oddly silent room and finally, she told me what she'd seen.

"That plaque had my father's name on it," she said, emotionlessly. "Someone donated this part of the hospital in his name."

She spoke infrequently of her father. She'd been sixteen when he died of a heart attack, sixteen when she learned the danger of love and the safety of walls. Having learned the same thing at twelve, I had always understood this. And now, reaching out with my very risky hand, I said, "I'm not going to die. I'm not going to leave you."

She came over to me, took my hand and then slowly, carefully, lay down at my side and cried into my shoulder.

Betty stops massaging my shoulders and searches my face and eyes. I try to repeat that promise now, try to put it into my eyes, and she catches it and kisses me as close to my lips as the respirator will allow.

There is a rush of noise and she is washed away by a wave of doctors who poke and prod, check numbers and shout orders. I hear words like "remarkable" and "terrific" while they speculate about unlikely complications. Their news is good, but still I feel fearful and anxious. One of them lifts my arm and it is so bruised that I can't believe it's mine. Then I shift my gaze a little, trying to pick up my reflection in the eyeglasses of the two doctors hovering over my head. I see a face impossibly swollen, resembling a balloon onto which someone has drawn a nose and a mouth and tiny swollen eyes. I turn to find the clock on the wall and I cannot believe there can possibly be five more minutes before my pain medication. Then I realize that this is how the rest of my life will be: tied down by my pain and my doctors and by the fear that anything could go wrong at any second. I start kicking and grabbing, trying to break free. They are injecting something into my IV bag, and I don't know what it is, all I know is that I am tired. I am tired of the pain and of trying to be good; I am tired of trying to accept all this. I am a prisoner and will never know freedom. The medication acts quickly and I am plunged into darkness.

"The problem is, I'm a chameleon," I said, shifting on the couch. "I become whoever I'm with. When I'm with you, I'm soft spoken and reasonable. When I'm with Candy, I'm street-smart and tough. When I'm with Lenny, I lisp and talk about what everyone is wearing. It's like I'm trying on other people's personalities to see how they fit. I don't want to do this, I want to be myself. I mean, where the hell is my personality?"

"You're experimenting," he said. "Give yourself a break. You're moving very fast. You'll find yourself."

"When?" I asked.

"Every morning that you wake up, you're more you than you were the day before."

That wasn't comforting; it was even a bit saccharine, and it was completely out of character for Dr. Brett. Since I'd been detoxed, I met with him three times a week in his cramped office. Dr. Brett was a small, balding, middle-aged, preppie-type who wore green or red ties with ducks on them and matching socks that barely covered his spindly ankles. When I first met him, I thought that his unnaturally even temper was due either to high enlightenment or heavy tranquilizers but I soon figured out that it merely indicated his supreme degree of tolerance of the world, and especially of his patients. We'd clashed more than a few times, and one time he even threatened to have the PET people—the psychiatric evaluation team—come in and drag me off to Camarillo, the state mental hospital. I knew I had to watch my step. Still, if I put aside what I felt about Dr. Brett personally, I had to admit that I was getting something out of these sessions.

"What about my mother?" I asked impatiently. "How do you think she fits into all of this?" He always brought up my mother at the precise moment when there was absolutely no need to, but I thought it politic to please him, though it didn't make much sense to me.

"What do you think?" he said.

"She never found herself. She spent her whole life looking and came up empty. Maybe I'm afraid that'll happen to me. Maybe I feel it's her fault that I'm so fucked up. If she hadn't died when she did, maybe I would've turned out better."

"Sounds good," he said, "but why would you have turned out better?"

"I was a kid! A baby! Man, after that, I was alone. *Alone!* She let me down."

"Right! She let you down! So how did that make you feel?" he asked.

"Angry," I said. "And guilty. I mean, how can you be angry at someone for dying? It wasn't her fault."

"It wasn't her fault but you're still allowed to be angry," he said.

"So I guess the guilt led to my drug use and suicide attempts, and if I forgive her and let the anger and guilt go, then my need to escape will disappear and I'll be happy?"

"*Yes!*" Dr. Brett looked really pleased with himself. "Yes," he said again.

"But that's just a theory, isn't it?" I said. "I mean, it's logical, but it's only words. I don't feel anything."

"Then how did you come to this?" he asked, disappointed.

"Candy spelled it all out for me in group the second day I was here. It makes sense, but so what?"

Dr. Brett leaned back in his chair.

"I didn't mean to put down what you're trying to do, or anything," I said. "I know you want me to figure out all that guilt stuff about my mother and to understand that the reason I don't much like or trust males is because of my father, but . . . I don't feel it, it's not *happening.*"

"Who talks like that, who says, 'it's not happening'?"

"Everybody here," I said, curious.

"Who says it the most and in just the way you said it?"

"Candy, I suppose," I said. I'd been acting like Candy; I'd assumed her toughness, her cynicism, her know-it-all attitude, and until now it had been effective, but something wasn't working anymore.

———

156

"Does Candy know more than I do?" he asked. I looked at all the degrees hanging on his walls and thought I'd better tread lightly around this question.

"She has a different knowledge. She's lived more than you."

"How do you know that?" he asked.

"It's an assumption," I said. I looked at the clock on the wall.

"You have a lot of assumptions," he said. "Where do they come from?"

"Living . . . they don't all come from my childhood."

"There are things we think are true because experience has borne them out, and then there are things we *know* are true," he said. "Dallas, what do you know?"

"*Know?* Like know, absolutely, positively?" I asked. He nodded.

"I know I'm hungry . . . and anxious. . . . I'm a good drummer. No, I don't know that anymore. . . . Ummm, isn't this a bit too philosophical for psychiatry?"

"What do you *know*?" he repeated, his face expressionless.

I hated that blank look of his, I mean, what was I, anyway? I stood and started pacing around the office. "I know. . . . I know . . . aren't we almost out of time?"

"Try sitting with your eyes closed," he said. I sat down in a chair and closed my eyes tightly. In the darkness I saw splashes of color moving in circles, then faces and scenes were flashing by, but too quickly to recognize, and then the image of my son floated in and stayed. I saw him clearly, sitting at my drums, poised to hit them with sticks as big as his arms. But the image was washed away by a rush of sharp painful feelings and when I opened my eyes I had to shake my head.

157

"I know that I have too much pain to live with," I said, "and I'm not saying that for effect. I believe that."

"Believing doesn't count," he said. "You don't *know* this."

I stood and paced again, in a very bad mood.

"I know that I hate going to bed at night," I was almost shouting. "I hate not having any sleeping pills because I lie awake for hours, afraid of what I'll see if I close my eyes." I stopped. This was the first time I'd admitted it to anyone, the first time I'd admitted it to myself—I needed to be smashed to close my eyes, I needed to be drugged to go to sleep.

"What else?" he said patiently.

"Don't you want to know what I'm afraid of looking at?" I asked. *Jesus.*

"We'll get there . . . what else do you know?"

"I like short cuts. I never take the sidewalk if I can cut across the lawn—that's something I know," I said.

"We're almost out of time," he said. "Try sitting down and closing your eyes again, and then answer the question."

"That is like opening the gates of hell, man," I said, stomping my foot. Then I felt embarrassed. "OK, that's an exaggeration, but . . . oh, all right, man. All right!" I sat back down, closed my eyes, held on tight to the arms of the chair, and braced myself for whatever horror would come.

An image of night, with a warm orange sunset fading in the distance. Then, careening at the speed of light through the darkness, came my 1973 blue Dino Ferrari, a real dream car that I had discarded on the shoulder of the Pacific Coast Highway over ten years ago. As I stood on a promontory above the ocean, the car approached; it maneuvered wildly through the air and then it hovered above me, the engine purring as it paused in the moonlit sky. The car eased closer, then it circled me, waiting for me to do something. But I hesitated and when I reached for the hood, the car reared back and headed off with purpose into the night. Soon it was just a glimmer above the horizon . . . then it was gone.

I opened my eyes. "I know that I lost my Ferrari," I said in surprise.

Dr. Brett allowed himself a slight smile. "Good," he said, as he stood up.

"Why would I think of that?" I asked. " What's 'good' about that? Why the fuck would something like that come into my mind?"

"See you tomorrow," he said.

"Tomorrow? What about the damned Ferrari?" I said.

"You tell me," he said, handing me a pen and a yellow legal pad. "Homework. Tell me about the Ferrari and make a list of what you know." Then he seemed to relax a bit and said, almost in a conversational tone, "But before you go, tell me why you didn't say a word today about Jill."

Somehow, I found it easy to answer him directly. "Because I'm seeing her tonight. I'm going AWOL and going to a New Year's Eve party with her."

"Give her my best," he said. "And be careful of the roads. There'll be a lot of drunk drivers tonight."

As I left Dr. Brett's office, I was wondering why he didn't take my AWOL seriously. I figured that at this point he knew more than I what I was capable of, and if he didn't believe my leaving was possible, then maybe it wasn't. Maybe I wouldn't be climbing out the window at 10:30 and jumping into the yellow Buick station wagon that would be waiting in the parking lot. Maybe I wouldn't be walking into Stephen's private party, uninvited and looking like a million bucks. I thought I was going. Maybe I would go, but Dr. Brett sure didn't think I was going, and Candy hadn't placed me on any special precautions, so I guessed I wasn't going. Maybe I'd call Jill and tell her not to come; then again, maybe I wouldn't. Well, I still had four hours to figure it out.

I walked down the hall to the TV lounge to have a cigarette and think about the assignment. Paolo was alone in the room, sitting in front of the TV, smoking and leafing through an AA book.

"What it be?" he asked, tucking the book under his leg.

"Need a butt bad," I said, lighting my cigarette. I sat on the stained blue couch and cradled my pad and pen, waiting for an idea.

"Your mother show?" I asked. Paolo shook his head.

"Didn't even call to make an excuse this time. I think I be blowing this place soon," he said.

"You can't change your family," I said, "but just because they let you down is no reason to get fucked up over it."

"You're sounding more and more like Mr. Program every day," he said.

"Can't let that fuck you up either. As for me, Paolo, it's the only life preserver around." Paolo picked up his book and held it out in front of him, looking at it from all angles and sides as if it were a treasure chest and he had to figure a way to break in. I put my things down and waved him over. He sat next to me and I took the book from him and opened it.

"Read," I said, pointing to a paragraph. He took a long, deep breath and fought an impulse to jump over the couch. He put his finger underneath the first word and sounded it out like a first grader. He stumbled over the next few words and came to a complete stop when he came to the word "together."

"Why didn't you tell me?" I asked him.

"I don't want no one to know," he said. "No one."

"This is nothing to be ashamed of," I said. "It's something that we can fix."

"Maybe you can help me," he was saying as John walked into the room. Paolo slammed the book shut and stuck it back under his leg. John fidgeted with his glasses and looked at us, his head cocked like a dog's, trying to understand.

"We were . . . doing an assignment," I said. Paolo nodded and looked at the floor. John walked over and sat on the couch with us. He was less thin and yellow since Elaine had left, but he was starving for something, and physical contact seemed to be his solution. He gave wrestler-grip hugs and was so contemptuous of the concept of personal space that he'd sit in your lap if you'd let him.

"May I help?" he asked. "Three heads are always better than two."

"No big deal," said Paolo, standing and walking to the TV set.

"It's something that we have to do ourselves," I said.

"I'm very good with the written word," he said. "I've got a degree in philosophy and English literature."

"You've got too much schooling to understand," said Paolo. He flipped through the channels fast. He liked John and wanted to tell him his secret.

"Hey, homeboy," I said. "If you wanted to learn how to throw a baseball, who would you go to? Fernando Valenzuela or some jerk that quit the high school team?"

"Shut up, man," Paolo said.

"Paolo, one thing I know is, if there's something you want, you can't let anything get in your way before you get it," I said.

"I want my mother to come here," he said, starting to cry. "I want her to come here for at least ten fucking minutes so she'll see what I'm doing and be proud. I want that and it ain't going to happen. I never get what I want, man."

"You can't change her, but you can change you. You want to fix yourself, then fucking do it. You want to stay in the fucking hole you're in, then stay there," I said. I was still acting like Candy.

"There's a subplot here that's escaping me," John said. Paolo walked over and sat between us on the couch. He picked up the book and opened it.

"I don't know how to read," he whispered while looking down at the floor.

"Want some help?" John asked. "I used to do some substitute teaching at a grade school in northern California." Paolo relaxed; he smiled and nodded. John took the book, flipped to the beginning, moved so close to Paolo that you couldn't fit a ruler between them, and then started the lesson. I picked up my pen and legal pad and wrote down the heading "Things I Know." I paused and watched John and Paolo for a minute and then I wrote my first two entries: "People need each other" and "I want to be a kind man."

I thought about it some more, but the image of the Ferrari interfered, and finally I just let it in and tried to interpret it. Candy would explain it as a representation of childish excess and irresponsibility, that it was a reminder of how bad things can get. I had, after all, lost the car because I was too strung out to care about it. More than once I'd nearly killed myself in it. The closest call I had was on the night I decided to see if I could fly it.

That was two years after I'd been fired from CSN, and about six months after I'd gotten together with Stephen for the first Manassas album. I had married Laura by then, who was as beautiful, sensual, understanding, and wild as ever. I had regained my position as a major rock drummer with the success of the album and the tour with Stephen and Manassas, and I had begun to moderate my cocaine and heroin use so that my doses hadn't increased for well over a month. Everything was moving along, but it was beginning to drag, and I got the urge to let it all go.

I'd read somewhere that some people were wired differently; they were born with a higher threshold for excitement and required practically life-threatening situations to get the same natural adrenalin high that so-called normal people get from a bike ride in the hills. So one evening while watching TV and coasting on a small hit of heroin, some coke, and a bottle of wine, I decided to test my own wiring. I was living on Mulholland then, in a house with jetliner views of the valley, and only a few minutes from Stephen, the Sunset Strip, and most major freeways. Laura was smoking something with a friend in the kitchen when I poked my head in and told her that I was going out for a drive. She nodded and her smile indicated that her sense of stagnation perfectly matched my own—I knew that she'd be at a club or party within ten minutes after I'd left. I went out the front door, jumped in the Ferrari, and headed toward the freeway.

The night was warm and filled with stars and saturated with the fragrance of night-blooming jasmine. I drove slowly at first to enjoy the evening and then started gunning it on the curves to make a blur of the lights below. I headed west to pick up the Ventura Freeway and thought I'd drive north along the coast until I got bored. At the on-ramp I picked up a blond hitchhiker named Jeff who was stoned and heading to San Francisco. He wore a leather shirt and a coonskin hat and said he was from Oregon and that CSN was his favorite band.

"Feel like flying?" I asked.

"Far out!" he said, as I stomped on the accelerator and started darting and weaving through the four northbound lanes. The windows were down and the wind was whipping in with such violence that conversation was impossible. We did eighty-five until I thought we were safely out of town and then I pumped it up to a hundred. Jeff was plastered against the seat, his mouth pulled back at the sides, his hair flat against his skull. As we pulled onto the Coast Highway and headed north, I pointed to the glove compartment. Jeff opened it, and pulled out a rig and a bag of cocaine.

"Fix it!" I screamed, thinking that I'd have to tell him how to do it. He calmly closed his window, expertly melted a mixture of heroin and coke with a cigarette lighter, and then sucked it all into the dirty syringe I kept underneath the seat. I eased off the accelerator, held out my right arm and with the delicacy of a nurse he tied it off with his headband and stuck the needle in a plump vein. He pulled back, filling the syringe with blood and then, while watching my eyes, he put full pressure on the plunger and slammed the juice home. The warmth started in my arm, moved to my chest, and at the exact moment that I expected to feel the head rush, I pushed the accelerator to the floor. The speedometer went as far to the right as space would allow just as my head exploded with color and pain. We were on a straightaway doing at least a hundred and forty and I thought I felt the wheels leave the pavement. I thought I saw clouds around us and stars within reach. I waited for the peace and fulfillment that I was sure only birds, God, and astronauts enjoyed, but felt nothing. The car would go no faster, and the test had ended in a sudden brain-splitting headache. I slowed down, got off at the next exit, and drove to a convenience store for a Dr. Pepper.

Maybe my mind dreamed up the car to remind me of all that, and to persuade me not to go AWOL and go back to all that—that's how Candy would explain it.

Dr. Brett, on the other hand, would probably talk about penises and potency and power, and he'd somehow bring my parents into it. They were both probably right, but these explanations gave me nothing. What I felt was hope, that somehow hope was returning in a blue Ferrari.

"He's right," John said to Paolo. "A man has to finally take responsibility for himself. Now read that again, slower, and sound everything out."

When I left the hospital in early 1985, no one but Candy really believed I had a chance. John and Paolo were supportive and offered as many perfunctory "I know you can do it's" as they could stomach, and Lenny just smiled and avoided the subject altogether. I wanted to stay sober and knew that I wouldn't live a year if I didn't, but I doubted that I had the strength. I'd successfully fought off hundreds of impulses to go AWOL or smuggle something into the hospital, but that had all been achieved while living in a controlled setting with a dozen mothers waiting to pick me up the moment I fell. I had no faith in my ability to say no to anything and was afraid of how empty and gray everything would seem without the glow and illumination of drugs. The world I was returning to was a bombed-out, desolate landscape littered with the carcasses of every personal and professional relationship I ever had. I had no career, a passionless marriage, no money, no place to live, and no real belief that I could change any of it.

"You can handle the depression," Candy said in my good-bye group. "We all live with it. Every minute of every day. You never learned to handle it because since you were twelve, you've been anesthetizing yourself the second you start to feel it. Now you'll learn to handle it or you'll die."

"Sure, it's no fun returning to the wreckage of your life but what's the alternative?" John said. "You're starting all over. This is day number one. I'm just glad it's you that got out first so there'll be someone out there to help me when it's my turn."

There were hundreds of hugs and promises and when the graduation ceremony was finished and all of the good-byes were over and all of the other patients were off in their groups and activities, Candy stood alone at the door waiting for me. I walked slowly down the hall because I wanted both to avoid and savor this moment; I felt as if I were leaving my mother.

"It's important to me that you succeed," she said, straightening my collar and dusting nothing off my shoulders. "I believe in you."

"Why?" I asked.

"You came along when I needed hope," she said.

"You don't really think I've got a chance, do you?"

"Sure as shit do," she said. "But get *into* recovery. Become an aide, answer a hotline, clean bedpans, anything. Get out of yourself for awhile. You find hope in other people and the things you do for them."

"I can't tell you how much you've helped me," I said. "I'm taking a lot of you with me."

"Well, pass me around," she said, giving me a final hug. "It won't be the first time."

I held her for a long time and then slowly left, feeling sad and terrified and fighting off an overwhelming urge to ask her to marry me or adopt me.

"That won't work," Dr. Brett had told me in our last session. "You can't keep trying to marry your mother."

"Why the hell not?" I said, a bit loudly. From the moment I'd walked into his office that morning, all my good feelings about the doctor had dissolved and I'd grown completely disenchanted with this preppy geek. He seemed smugger than ever and I was hoping he'd say something really stupid so I could walk out on him.

"For the same reason that you can't continue to pick fights with every male authority figure you meet. Your father is gone. Your mother is gone." He had a vein on his forehead that pulsated whenever I started a fight with him — my father had had the same vein — and I could not help wanting to pop it.

"So what?!" I said, even more loudly. He took a deep breath and wiped his face with his hand.

"So why do you want to make this last session so difficult?" he asked. "Is it easier to say goodbye in anger?"

"It's not hard to say goodbye to you, no matter what mood I'm in," I said. Then Dr. Brett folded his arms and turned away from me in his swivel chair.

"Remember when you were paranoid," he said, "when you felt that there was someone outside waiting to get you? Did that person have a face?"

The question surprised me and I saw it as a distraction, but it made me nervous. I couldn't see his face, so I didn't know where he was going

"Did this person ever have a face?" he continued evenly, not turning around. I did not want to start in with this stuff, but this guy was signing my discharge forms so, reluctantly, I thought about it. I tried to remember the face from my fears and my dreams, but I could see nothing clearly.

"It didn't," I finally said, "but there was a feeling . . ."

"What was that?" he asked.

"My mother . . . my father . . . I never understood why they'd make me afraid."

"Why would they make you feel afraid?" he asked.

"I just said, I didn't understand that. Turn around and look at me, man," I said.

"Why would they make you afraid?" he persisted, his back still to me. My anger was dissolving and the paranoia I'd put away weeks ago had returned.

"Because . . . they're waiting for me?" I said.

"Waiting for you?" he asked.

"Waiting for me. Waiting for me to join them. To die."

"To die? Is there any escape from them?" he asked.

"What the hell difference does it make? Why do you shrinks always bring it back to mom and dad?"

"I didn't," he said. "You did. Tell me what you *know*."

I closed my eyes to see or feel an answer. The room was warm and dusty and I could hear the muffled sounds of the patients in the hall. The pain in my stomach that had started the day before became sharper and my hands felt cold. In the darkness I concentrated on seeing my parents and the images came swiftly. There were delicate, early memories of my mother, young and smiling, pushing me on a swing, then sitting on it while I pushed; my father tall in his uniform, shifting from foot to foot, then sitting in the backyard in shirt-sleeves, drinking iced tea. Then the scenes shifted to something darker and I saw the lines around my mother's mouth and eyes deepening; my father sitting alone in the dark living room; my mother, weeping and clinging to his leg as he choppily moved packed bags to the door. Then my mother lying still, platinum hair and white flesh and worn sheets, a living ghost who had become a real one; my father's cockpit, split into sharp pieces and spattered with blood.

"No," I said finally, "there's no escaping it.

"You're a prisoner," he said without inflection. "A doomed man."

"Well, yes, I see myself like that."

"Who created the prison?" he asked. I was dying to see his face. I wanted to grab his chair and spin it around.

"My parents? I'm the product of their genes and fuck-ups," I said.

"So's your sister. She's never had your problems," he said.

"So, OK," I said. "I guess it's me. It's got to be me, right?"

"That would be my guess," he said, slowly turning toward me.

"What is this, man? Your face is some fucking reward for coming up with the right answer?"

"If I hadn't turned away, you would have kept getting angrier and would have stayed focussed on that. You proba-bly would have walked out of the session early, but you didn't and, in fact, we're ten minutes over."

"I was planning on walking out on you," I said, amazed.

"Your anger would have made all of these past few minutes impossible," he said. I thought I caught a glimpse of approval in his face.

"I create my own prison," I repeated, almost to myself, not sure of what I felt about all this. I did know that the pain in my belly was gone and my hands were no longer cold.

"That would be my guess," he said, standing. "And you are the only one who can set yourself free."

"That sounds like AA talk," I said, putting my hand out to shake his.

"Sometimes we talk alike," he said, taking my hand and shaking it awkwardly.

And so I left the unit. I had nothing but thirty days of sobriety and the knowledge that this was my last chance. Failure this time would mean death, and I wanted desperately to believe I had some control over that.

8

The Party

"The chief functions of the liver are to cleanse the blood of toxins that creep in daily and to ensure that the body has enough blood to keep it going. . . . The liver is one of the easiest organs to transplant. . . . Seventy-five percent of those who survive the surgery live at least a year; if you make it that long the chances of living for five years is also about seventy-five percent. Cyclosporins are new drugs that act like a friendly AIDS virus by impairing the immune system just enough to keep the body from rejecting the new liver. They can damage the kidneys and cause seizures. . . . Steroids do the same thing to the immune system but are less good at it and will make the face puffy and can cause uncontrollable mood shifts. Over the long term they can cause bone disease and diabetes. You will have to take both of these medications for the rest of your life."

Betty pauses to see if I want her to continue. She is reading notes that I kept from my reading and from the information sessions given by the transplant team. I have forgotten almost all of this and I write on my chalkboard "go on." So she does. . . .

"After surgery you will be in the ICU for an average of three days and hospitalized for an average of three weeks. You will be susceptible to infections and must not have visitors who are sick or who have been exposed recently to someone who is.

"Law forbids that we tell you anything about your donor but should you wish to thank the family we suggest an unsigned letter, which we will deliver for you."

I signal her to continue but there is no more. Her voice is so comforting and distracting so I point to another notebook which is filled with stuff I was working on just before the transplant. She picks it up and leafs through it.

"Notes for the book. Do you want me to read these?" she asks. I nod yes, and she takes them out and begins reading.

It started with a phone call from Astrid Wyman. She was inviting me to a party she was throwing for Bill Wyman her ex-what? lover? common-law husband? I had known Astrid and Bill for almost twenty years, and even the thought of seeing them again was exciting and I immediately said yes. The party was to be in several weeks when the Stones were in town on tour and it would be at Eric Gardner's house; Eric was Bill's manager.

Betty may have felt a bit wary, given my history with Astrid, but she was keenly aware of my increasing burn-out working in recovery, and my resurgent desire to make music, and she, too, immediately said yes. We both felt that five years clean and sober had made me stronger, wiser, more disciplined and self confident, and we were eager to show the new Dallas to everyone.

I had met Bill in Miami, where Stephen and I were working on the first Manassas album at a new studio called Criteria. Eric Clapton had just finished recording the *Derek and the Dominoes* album there, and the studio came highly recommended. One night we ran into Bill at a party and invited him to play with us and he promised he'd join us at the studio in a few days.

"Hey, man, wouldn't it be cool if we could get Bill to quit the Stones and join us?" Stephen had a big shit-eating grin on his face as he said this, but he was only half-joking. . . . Then we came to our senses. "Na-a-ah!" we said simultaneously. "Never happen!"

It was a typical Florida summer, with temperatures of eighty-five degrees at midnight and humidity that stayed at ninety percent. I felt like I was trying to breathe underwater. I hated it; it reminded me of Texas. The air was so muggy the cocaine gummed up; it was like trying to snort Silly Putty.

"Hey, D! Bill Wyman is on his way over to the studio to play with us," Stephen said a couple of days later.

"Fuck, man," I muttered, trying to pack my nose as best I could. As I lifted my head out of the plastic bag full of soggy coke, Bill Wyman walked in, closely followed by Astrid, a stunning blond Swede who spoke English without the heavy accent that usually made me laugh. Stephen and I had just recorded a track called "Love Gangster." It was really just a jam, but when Bill picked up the bass and started playing, everything came together. We could do no wrong. It was take one and it kicked ass. I was so loaded that at the end of the tune I dropped my sticks and started laughing, but even that sounded good and Stephen left it on the record. We all worked so well together, but Stephen kept his head and didn't ask Bill to leave the Stones.

Years later, Bill confided to me that he had been really disappointed that day when we didn't ask him to join Manassas. As comical as it sounds, Bill had been feeling fed up with the Stones and was ready for a change. Another opportunity to make rock and roll history fallen by the wayside.

Bill and I remained good friends throughout the years. I played on two of his solo albums and whenever we were in the same city, we partied together, but in the end my self-destructiveness drove him away, as it did nearly everyone else. He hung around much longer than most, and tried as hard as Stills to pull me out of my nosedive, but finally he could watch no more. I hadn't seen him since he had kicked me out of his house almost ten years ago.

On the night of Astrid's party we spent too much time dressing while simultaneously downplaying the importance of the event. Rolling Stones parties always brought out the power people and rock royalty, so the opportunity to show the music community that I was alive, thriving, and eminently employable was a golden one. It was all a bit nerve-racking, so Betty and I invited some friends to go with us for support: a Los Angeles Raider named Newt, who was one of the largest human beings I've ever seen; his tiny wife Spunky, who was one of the cutest; and George, a psychiatrist we knew through our work who was a major Stones fan.

It was a warm, clear night. We arrived at the high-walled, sprawling estate reasonably late and waited only a minute at the gate while security checked our names on the list. The huge Spanish-style mansion clung to the side of a mountain and had spectacular ocean-to-city views. We could hear music and laughter floating up from somewhere at the back of the house, and as we descended the staircase to the front door, we could look through the tall windows and see large, colorful rooms filled with people. When we finally reached the front door, I hesitated. I was certain that I could handle being around drugs and alcohol and people who still believed that they were an answer; I was reasonably confident that I would be able to deal with all the envy I was sure to feel seeing people I'd started out with who were now legends. But I was terrified of running into people I'd hurt, deserted, disappointed, or embittered, and as this represented most of the people in the music industry, there was sure to be some unpleasantness ahead.

The tall doors swung open, letting a group of severely dressed young men out, and I led my group in. Standing just inside, acting the perfect hosts, were Eric Gardner and his wife, Janis. He was thin, crisply dressed, very tan, and very polite; she was blond, voluptuous, and wore a dress that probably required a mortgage. Eric had the reputation of being one of the few truly good people in the music business. He was a perfectionist and he kept his client list small so he could do the job he required of himself: it included the likes of Bill, Elvira, Timothy Leary, the Stray Cats, and Todd Rundgren.

Though we were merely acquaintances, Eric and Janis greeted us as if we were schoolmates and ushered us into the living room.

The room was filled with art and exquisite furnishings and an attractive crowd that seemed remarkably young. Eric introduced us to a few people, complimented me on my days with CSN, pointed to where we could find food and drinks, and then returned to his post at the front door. Newt headed for the food, George for the bar, and I searched for a familiar face.

I had been off the A-list for parties since Nixon was president, a time when most of the people around me would have been in nursery school, and I was surprised at how tame they had become. There would be no furniture throwing or fist fighting with these young Beverly Hills-types unless I started it and, as my goals for the evening were forgiveness and acceptance, this was extremely unlikely.

Betty pulled me toward a line of people exiting through the French doors at the back of the house and I followed. Then I caught a glimpse of someone I recognized. Sitting alone on a couch was a tiny, blond, beautiful girl dressed all in black. No name came to mind, but she was so familiar that I reasoned she had to be an ex-patient of mine. So with Betty in tow, I headed over toward her. Halfway there Betty pulled me to a stop as the girl stood and like a frightened deer, disappeared from the room.

"Lisa Marie Presley," Betty said, steering me back toward the French doors.

"Are you sure? She looked so familiar," I said.

"We buy too many cheap magazines," she said.

The French doors opened onto a narrow staircase leading down to a wide expanse of lawn covered with rented tables and chairs. The yard ended at a flight of steps that in turn led down a hill to a fountain and gardens, that opened onto an extraordinary view of the city. At least a two-million-dollar view, I figured; two million-five if there was a pool or a tennis court. I started thinking about how easily I could have bought a place like this in the early seventies, before the California land boom, and then I started thinking how every room we'd seen so far, including the kitchen, was larger than our studio apartment. Envy started rising in me like I had spoiled fish for lunch.

Betty studied the layout of the yard, carefully selected an unoccupied table, and planted herself in one of the aluminum chairs facing the crowd. Years of watching her mother give political fundraisers had taught her the art of strategic seating, and I sat next to her realizing several beats later that this table not only ensured high visibility but also easy access. People will say hello to almost anyone if it's clear they're on their way somewhere else and so they don't have to commit to a conversation.

"Feel like something to drink?" she asked, scanning the crowd. They were older down here, less perky, and not as perfectly dressed, yet just as tame. Definitely a Hollywood A-list party, with lots of famous people from movies and television in addition to the music industry. Peter Falk and Tiffany, an overnight singing sensation, were seated at the table next to us. Falk was talking loudly to some old hippie and, from the way he slurred his words and swayed, appeared drunk and the exception to the rule. Tiffany sat silently, surrounded by some older people who had to be chaperones. She seemed very uncomfortable, poured into a dress that tried to make her look old enough to menstruate.

"Yeah, I'd like an Evian," I said to Betty.

"Me, too. I think the bar is over there," she said, pointing to the end of the house. I stood slowly, a little uneasy about striking out alone this soon.

"I'll have one, too," a male voice said. "With ice and lime." I turned and saw Rob Lowe greeting Betty as he took my seat. He was a good friend of Betty's younger brother, Brad, and a casual friend of ours. I shook his hand, grateful to see a friendly face from our everyday life, and left them to their gossip while I headed off on my own.

The light was dim and the faces in the crowd were sometimes difficult to make out. I waved to Graham, only to discover a minute later that it wasn't him, but John Mayall. I was about to say hello to Astrid, when I discovered she was twenty years too young and holding the hand of Alice Cooper. I had known Alice since I first started out. As a kid in Phoenix, I had played with two of his original band members. I remember busting a gut when they told me they were going to name their band "Alice Cooper" to make fun of Al Kooper, who at the time was getting a hell of a lot of what we thought was undeserved attention. I hesitated before touching him on the back because suddenly I couldn't remember his nonstage name, and when I saw that he was talking to Eric Clapton, who was leaning against a wall slightly in the shadows, I panicked and disappeared into the crowd.

I had no reason to do this. I'd first met Eric in the late sixties when Stephen and I were in England. We had just finished the first CSN album and had flown to London to try to recruit a bass player and a keyboardist—three singers and a drummer do not a band make. It was my first trip to England and I loved everything about it except for the cocaine we got there, which smelled bad and tasted funny. Also I found it difficult to snort coke while driving on the wrong side of the road—it made me carsick.

Anyway, we were staying in London, practicing and planning who we'd like to ask to be part of the band, and we were making regular forays into a countryside that was practically littered with major British talent. I remember one trip we made to Olympic Recording Studios to listen to a bass player someone had told us about. That didn't work out, so Stephen and I looked around for a bit, wandering from room to room, just to see what was going on. As we entered one of the rooms we heard a gravel voice roar out through the soundproof glass: "She came in through the bathroom window!" I looked through the glass and saw this guy who appeared to be having convulsions.

I almost panicked, thinking, "God, somebody get in there and shove a spoon in his mouth before he swallows his tongue!" But no one else seemed fazed by his behavior and I managed to keep quiet; it wouldn't be cool to panic.

Then I heard a voice at my shoulder say, "Is this a closed session, then?" I turned and saw the voice belonged to George Harrison — George-fucking-Harrison! It got even harder to be cool.

"How d'you like my new discovery?" George asked Stephen. "His name is Joe Cocker. I found him hanging around the studio. I think he did the sweeping up or something."

"Take four," said the engineer. "Could you put a little more feeling in the next one, Joe?" Any more feeling and he'll explode, I thought.

Then we had a particularly unsuccessful visit with Stevie Winwood. We showed up at his house during a rainstorm, wired, soaking wet, and covered with mud, and proceeded to convince him of our desirability by playing too soon and too poorly. He politely said goodnight and locked himself in his bedroom. Undeterred and probably appearing quite insane, we stayed anyway, convinced in our increasing stupor that our noise would make him change his mind. It didn't, and we left the next morning saying our good-byes to a silent bedroom door, certain that he'd made a bad decision. Later we agreed that perhaps our approach needed improvement.

Several days later we showed up at Eric Clapton's less wired and much more in tune. The drive from London to Eric's house took about two hours, and Stephen's Ferrari sailed along over the lush and winding roads. As I stared out the window, I wondered why I'd heard that England is always rainy and gray. The sun was bright and the air was crisp and I thought to myself, "If my mama could see me now!"

We arrived at Eric's lavish country manor house and a slim, elegant, and very familiar looking woman answered the door, saying, "Come in . . . Eric will be right with you." As she spoke I realized that this was Patty Harrison, George's ex-wife, or soon to be ex, and that at a party a few days earlier this same woman had passed me a note that said she thought I was cute and could we get together? I had been too tongue-tied to respond, and of course I did not mention it now, but I did think, "Jesus, what next?"

Eric's house was *huge,* and ancient. I wasn't used to being in houses that were hundreds of years old. My cowboy boots were making loud echoing noises as we walked through the large entranceway, which made me very self-conscious and I found myself walking on my tiptoes.

"What are you going to say to him, Stephen," I whispered as we stood in the hall.

"I'm going to ask him to join the band, Dallas. What do you think we drove all the way out here for?" The question obviously irritated him.

"Cool, man," I said sheepishly.

After that exchange, Stephen and I didn't say another word to each other while we waited. Stephen paced and I stayed in one spot. Suddenly I caught myself staring at the cracks in the wall, just like David Geffen had told me to do when I first met him. It must have been close to an hour before Eric walked through the door.

Eric came in looking unshaven and disheveled. He was polite, but distant, and then he warmed up a bit. He and Stephen got to chatting and somehow the subject turned to

Ferraris. Eric got this big smile on his face and said, "Come with me, mates, I've got something to show you."

We followed him outside and walked past the garden to a large garage. He opened the door and there, on blocks, displayed like some precious *objets d'art*, were several of the most beautiful Ferraris I had ever seen. Our jaws dropped and for once it was OK to abandon being cool as Stephen and I let out simultaneous whoops of admiration: "Gee, wow!" "Golly!" "Oh, boy!"

Then Eric brought us back inside because he wanted to show Stephen his guitar collection. Eric and Stephen picked up guitars and started playing together and I beat out a rhythm with a pair of maracas that were lying around. Now, Stills was a very good guitar player; in fact, at that point in my career, I'd played with only one better — Jimi Hendrix. But I was soon to find out why people were referring to Eric as "God"; his playing was indeed impressive. Always a fierce competitor, Stephen took off after him, but there was no catching up, let alone staying with him. It was soon clear to me that Eric's joining CSN wasn't in the cards.

We left the guitar room, and it was time for more serious matters. Eric and Stephen went off to some part of the house and I went out and hung around in the garden. I couldn't believe that Stephen would actually have the guts to pop the question, and it wasn't long before Stephen reappeared, walking fast, and looking very pissed off. I knew it was best not to ask, but I asked anyway: "What happened, man?"

"He turned us down. Let's just get the fuck out of here." I thought there was something more, but decided to leave it alone. The ride back to London was quiet and heavy; I just stared out the window.

I'd seen Eric a few times since that initial interaction: years later he played with us on Stephen's solo album, on a song called "Go Back Home." We hung out doing a lot of cocaine, booze, and pot at that session, which went into the early morning hours. But I hesitated going up to him now out of fear that he wouldn't remember me. I was certain that later in the evening when I worked up the courage to say hello, he'd be a gentleman and say all of the proper things while staring blankly at me. Hopefully, later in the evening I wouldn't mind, but right now I needed a sure thing. I needed someone to reassure me that there was a time when I was somebody, and that my memories were not grandiose delusions born of youth and drugs.

I turned and saw Betty still at the table with Rob. Stephen Stills had joined them, and beside him was his gorgeous wife, Annie, an ex-model with unusual and beautiful Asian features. I was pleased to see her there because she usually does not like parties. Then I turned and pushed on through the crush gathered at the center of the yard, looking for Bill. I saw lots of people from the movie industry who looked familiar: the guy who starred in *Harold and Maude* talking to Katey Segal, that red-haired woman who plays the wife on *Married With Children*; the skinny woman who looks just like Olive Oyl and had that "Faerie Tale Theatre" series on cable sitting next to Little Richard and talking to an overweight Dennis Quaid.

On the edge of the crowd was Timothy Leary. He was dressed like a professor and stood with his arms crossed, talking with someone who seemed to understand whatever it was he was saying. When I was just getting sober, the very thought of this guy advocating drugs the way he did enraged me, and I enjoyed blaming my mistakes on him and his type.

Somewhere along the way I came to understand that they were just as gullible and empty as everyone else, and were guilty of nothing more than looking for a quick answer, like everyone else.

Leary gesticulated suddenly into the air, scaring someone half his size who seemed to have been hiding behind him. Holding a glass uncomfortably, the daughter of "The King" darted toward the cover of a fat lady in a ridiculous dress standing a few feet away. Then I remembered a story featured in one of those cheap tabloids that said this girl had just become a mother herself. The thought of someone so tiny, young, fragile, and seemingly alone having a baby was too sad to think about, and I pushed ahead toward the bar.

Once at the bar, I realized that the line of people waiting for a drink twisted back through the crowd, so I retraced my steps and took my place at what appeared to be the end of the line. As I stood there, someone touched my hand, and I turned and saw it was Astrid. She pressed her lips to my cheek.

"You came," she said, smiling and stepping slightly back to get a look at me. She was thin and tan and had the same long blond hair. Her uncommon beauty had peaked, but she could still stop a heart just by entering a room.

"I told you I would," I said. "You look . . . beautiful."

"You are such a nice boy," she said, hugging me. "Are you having a good time?" Her smell and the silkiness of her hair catapulted me back to the first time I slept with her. It was a warm night with a slight breeze and she stood by an open window dressed in a sheer, white gown. The wind blew her hair over what had to be the most perfectly formed breasts in the world. I remember thinking I could check this out in the morning by going through Bill's photo collection of

185

breasts — allegedly containing a picture of every pair that had ever entered his house. Then I remember her kissing me and the room starting to spin.

"I . . . brought my wife," I said, pointing to Betty, who chose this moment to look up. "I got married again."

"You were always doing that," she said as a woman touched her on the shoulder and whispered urgently into her ear. "She looks lovely."

"We're very happy," I said. Astrid gave me a disbelieving look and started walking away with the woman.

"Enjoy yourself," she said, indicating with a shrug and a roll of the eyes that something silly had to be attended to. "We'll talk later."

I watched her slice through the crowd and then I saw Betty watching me watch her. I smiled and turned back toward the line but I felt a sudden need to rejoin Betty as soon as possible, so I decided to cut. I walked around to the side of the bar, waved down a teenager whose only job appeared to be minding the supply of ice, asked him to get three bottled waters and in a minute was back at the table with Betty and Rob.

"I was getting pretty thirsty," Betty said.

"Astrid," I said.

"I gathered that," she said.

I hugged Stephen hello. He was moving to the other side of the table to talk football with Newt and I sat down in his seat.

"We're trying to figure out what's worth pursuing tonight," Betty said, indicating Rob. Betty has a wry sense of humor, and she was referring to Rob's recent troubles with a teenager and a video camera. Rob nodded and smiled, but kept his eyes on the crowd.

186

"I think Tiffany would be perfect," Betty said. "Just so we could watch the faces of those chaperones."

Three mini-skirted groupie types paused in front of the table and started giggling and posing to catch Rob's attention. They were attractive by most men's standards, but too obvious and aggressive and his face got steely and he turned away. I had seen the same face on Astrid countless times, when men threw themselves at her, and it occurred to me then that Rob and Astrid must be fucked up in ways fundamentally different from the rest of us. So much of who I am was formed by my correctly or incorrectly perceived physical deficiencies. I mean, why does anyone make the choices they do in life — their job, their appearance, their hobbies — but to appear attractive or desirable or to avoid facing that they're not? What would it be like to know from the very beginning that you are attractive and desirable? As I mulled this over, Rob started talking to Betty about movies, so I put this question to George, who had just sat next to me. He's a level-headed psychiatrist who's been on sabbatical, and has been spending his time reading and writing.

"First off, I'd say that no one is ever really convinced of anything," he said, not really interested in the question. "Self-doubt is universal and maybe the only reason for ambition and creativity. But the big question is, Who cares and what difference does it make? So, tell me about Astrid."

I laughed and wondered if I was dealing with guilt about my attraction to Astrid or jealousy at all the attention Rob was getting. Or maybe it was some kind of self-congratulation that after everything I'd been through, I was at last capable of thought and thoughtful words, although at the moment they did not interest George. I filed it all away to look at on Monday with my shrink, Dr. Thomas Trott.

———

When I first met Bill and Astrid, Astrid was very young, like the girl Bill had just married. But I didn't really get to know Astrid until I went to stay with them at their villa in the south of France. At the time, I was still in the early stages of getting strung out, but I couldn't get a job and anything I could steal or hock went into dope. When one of my dealers tried to poison me with bad heroin because I'd become a pain in the ass — things are really bad when your dealer tries to kill you — I decided I had to get out of Los Angeles and get my life back together. I called dozens of old friends for help and Bill was the only one who even bothered to return my call. Bill is truly a kind and decent man — and sensible. Reportedly, he's squirreled away every dime he ever made. Bill is known for his collections and over the years he has devoted many loving hours to putting together one of the most extensive blues libraries in the world. Bill's response to my call was to send me airfare and say I was welcome to stay with him and Astrid for as long as I liked.

My first stay was pretty unremarkable. Their house had been built by Russian royalty and it had spectacular views and a chapel and cloisters and was filled with incredible antiques. Bill was always off somewhere or sequestered in some room with his blues recordings, and so I spent most of my days by the pool drinking, trying to get off the dope, and watching Astrid. She was friendly, but distant. She was also drop-dead gorgeous and I probably would have sacrificed my last remaining friendship for five minutes alone with her, but she was devoted to Bill and never gave me even a hint that anything but polite conversation was possible. I left about two months later, tanned, less addicted to heroin, more addicted to alcohol, and hopeful that a lead I had for work would pan out. Well, it didn't, and I got more into heroin and more

188

desperate and so like any smart cat, I looked up my last meal. Bill was just as eager to help and again sent me airfare, but this time he suggested that I bring along my wife, Laura.

We arrived shabby and dirty, even for hippies, and then one night, after about a week of good food, lots of sun, and some new clothes, Bill suggested at dinner that we try wife swapping. It was Astrid's birthday and he said maybe I'd like to take her upstairs and give her a present.

After Laura and I got married, we both knew that we'd never stopped fooling around, but we'd never been open or honest enough to actually discuss it, so this would be a new, even liberating experience. I knew that Laura would go along and so instead of looking at her for the OK, I looked at Astrid. She smiled seductively and I will never forget that feeling. I mean, I felt like I hadn't had anything but bad luck for years, now suddenly I was the luckiest guy in the world. This was a face and a body that launched armadas and inspired sonnets and never gave a bum like me a second look. Well, Laura agreed and I gave Astrid her birthday present that night and as often as I was allowed for the next few months. Finally the excitement began to wear off for Bill and the possibility of another job came up for me, so Laura and I departed renewed and hopeful.

Predictably, over the next few months things got worse. I got more strung out, more broke, and pretty soon Bill's was the only phone number I knew and I was calling it constantly. One day he was dumb enough to answer it and I begged my way into another invitation. I made plans to be the best house guest anyone ever had so that I'd never have to leave.

Laura and I had split up by then, and since I knew that more than half the reason for the invitation was Laura, as a substitute I invited a woman named Mary who I had just started seeing. When we showed up, I was looking bad, I mean, real bad, as fat as I'd ever been, and Mary was not as attractive as Laura, so from the very first I knew this wasn't going to go well.

And it was soon apparent that no amount of sun, sleep, or good food was going to make the two of us any more desirable, and no overtures for sex came from Bill or Astrid. Just as I thought, the visit went poorly.

It was also becoming obvious that things were not going well between Bill and Astrid, and she was getting more and more depressed. Then one evening, at a party at a friend's house, Astrid slipped off into a bathroom and cut her wrists. They brought her to the emergency room of a local hospital and from there she was taken to a psych hospital where she was kept under observation for a few days. After this Bill became almost completely reclusive and spent his time obsessively working on his collections.

In the meantime, I was getting louder, meaner, more demanding, and basically turning into the houseguest-from-hell. My envy of Bill's success and his ability to manage it as calmly and responsibly as he did was raging out of control. I walked through the house endlessly, aching for confrontation, but everyone avoided me including the help. Then one night, while out on the town drunk and stoned out of my mind, I picked up a pretty young French woman in a restaurant and invited her back to the villa. I snuck her into the house and I found an out-of-the-way room downstairs and had sex with her on a new white couch Astrid had bought. After we finished, I passed out, and when I woke up the girl was gone and Astrid's couch looked as if someone had butchered a pig on it. An hour later on the way to the airport I learned that the girl was very, very young and was the daughter of a prominent local family. Bill changed his phone number and I hadn't seen him since.

"Does he know you're sober?" George asked.

"The word got around," I said.

"It's really hard to believe you're the same person," George said. "When you guys swapped, did you ever do it, together?"

"You mean me and Bill? No, I've never been into that. Bill either, as far as I know. We would fuck the girls on the same bed together, though. I used to get the sense that Bill disapproved of a lot of things Mick did. Mick used to fuck anything that moved and it almost tore the group apart more than a few times. I think something might've gone on between Mick and Astrid."

"Are you guys still talking about sex?" Betty asked, putting her arm on mine and turning toward us. Rob was talking to Graham Nash, who had just arrived with his wife, Susan.

"Talking about perspective and how easy you can lose it," George said.

"What's your perspective on tonight?" she asked me.

"Ask me later. Still too caught up to answer," I said. I already knew that the answer would not lie in renewed acceptance by this old world; it would be found in my own acceptance of my new world as more vital and important than the old. But this was not yet within my grasp, and Bill was in some way crucial to this resolution and I'd not yet seen him here.

"We can leave any time," Betty said.

"No, I'm fine. I'm actually having fun," I said.

We sat quietly then, watching the people. Carol Kane, who I loved so much from *Taxi* reruns, ran by wearing a heavy coat and dark sunglasses, and Gene Simmons from Kiss stood in line for potato salad. Phil Spector, looking the same as he always has, right down to the sunglasses and suit, roamed the outskirts of the crowd, occasionally nodding and waving but only rarely speaking. The notorious recluse crossed paths with that other party ghost, Lisa Marie. They bumped into, then ignored each other completely and went their separate ways with feigned purpose.

Stephen sat down at my right, friendly, stone-cold sober, and unusually undistracted.

"Not like the old parties," he said nostalgically, shaking his head. "I'm surprised they even let old farts like us in."

"Senior statesmen," I said, striking a noble pose. This thought sent him into a fit of laughter. Then his wife touched him on the shoulder and they got up from the table to speak privately. Betty got up too, and left to find a bathroom. Then George turned nervously and pointed with his head toward the stairs, indicating that someone important had just arrived. I turned and saw Joni Mitchell walking slowly toward our table, alone, looking unchanged, and smoking a cigarette; she was always smoking a cigarette.

David Crosby was seeing Joni when I'd first met her, and I was immediately impressed by her dignity and manners. Shortly afterwards, she was seeing Graham, and he would invite me up to her house in Laurel Canyon for tea, conversation, and instruction in art. Graham was probably the first person to realize that a lot of my shyness was due to inadequate schooling, and he took it upon himself to change this when our schedule lightened up. We would sit and sip tea at Joni's house, discussing politics and vocabulary and art. Graham introduced me to the work of Magritte, Dali, M.C. Escher, and other artists, and we talked about the choices they'd made in color and form, what these choices represented and how this translated into their particular world view.

Then at some point Joni would appear and start to play the piano and Graham would eventually join her. Sometimes they divided up the keyboard and played silly, childhood songs; other times their voices soared and interwove in something new she was writing. I thought they made the perfect couple, elegant, well educated, and gifted. I found myself becoming more curious about everything, more aware, and I looked forward to these afternoons all week.

One bright, sunny day I arrived at Joni's house too early for school and could find no one there. Thinking they'd be back soon, I stayed, wandering from room to room looking at photographs, instruments, wildflowers, and I was about to sit at the piano when Joni appeared from around a corner, stark naked. We were both surprised but only I felt embarrassed and I averted my eyes. She found what she was looking for and she left the way she came, and I took a furtive glance at her perfect ass. Innocent, natural, and almost certainly accidental, the incident left me with a vague sense of impotence. Stephen or David or Graham would not have acted the way I did. They created and seized opportunity. School stopped shortly after that when the band's schedule got hectic and I waited years for any door she might open even a crack, but it never happened.

Quite a long time after that, when my image had changed from that of the "kid next door" to something darker and more menacing, I ran into Joni and she asked if she could draw my face. I said sure, and she made some quick sketches and disappeared. It was a long time before I saw the finished piece, which was impressionistic and painted in dark, swirling colors that she said represented inner conflict and portended much struggle and pain. The painting is in a book somewhere.

"Introduce me," George said nervously. She had paused at the table before ours and hopefully we were next.

Betty was back. "You gotta see this," she said, grabbing my shoulder. "Rob is talking to Tiffany and the chaperones are grasping their chests." We laughed.

I turned to this scene, but I kept Joni in the corner of my eye. I felt both relieved and anxious when she headed straight for me.

I caught her eyes as she caught mine and saw they were warm with recognition.

"Dallas, it's been so long," she said, taking my hand and looking deeply at my face.

"Joni, it's so great to see you," I said confidently. Her hair was long and thinner and cut the same way. Instead of leaving wrinkles, time had somehow pulled the flesh of her face more taut, giving it a healthy, weathered look. Her body was larger, but solid, and her long, expressive fingers were as beautiful as ever.

"You look very good," she said, about to move on. I quickly introduced Betty and Newt and Spunky, and when she came to George she held his hand for a minute searching for something in his eyes. She left abruptly without an explanation. I felt very good.

"What the hell was she looking for?" George asked.

"Your vibes, your soul, a positive ID as the guy who stole her purse last week? Who cares and what difference does it make?" I said.

"It's getting late," Betty said. We'd have to be up at five for work and I'd been so tired lately, she was already anticipating the battle she'd have with me in the morning.

"A few more minutes," I said, searching the crowd for Bill, the one person I still wanted to see.

Groups of people carrying plates piled high with expensive food were claiming tables all around us, and though we weren't particularly hungry, George was dispatched to the buffet.

By the time George got back, a familiar, small, thin, steady form was moving through the crowd. Between the plates he was juggling and the number of greetings he had to return, he was walking slowly, but Bill was walking toward me.

Betty and George could see my nervousness and tried unsuccessfully to humor me out of it. Bill was coming closer and closer and then he was at my table, asking if he could join us. I was on my feet immediately and went to hug him, which he accepted in his formal British way. Then, like Astrid, he stepped back to get a good look at me. The years had made Bill appear a bit thinner, but otherwise he was unchanged. I held out my hand to him, he grasped it, and tweaked my nose with his free one, as if I were his kid brother.

I introduced Betty and my friends and we sat and spoke of nothing at first: how well the Stones tour was going, how much older and taller our children had gotten. I then told him of my sobriety and of my job and he seemed genuinely pleased and spoke jokingly of his recent marriage and that his son was, indeed, older than his bride.

"Did you get your passes and tickets to the concert?" he asked, smiling.

"Yes, thanks," I said, nodding. Just then Little Richard sat down next to Bill and they picked up on a conversation that obviously had started a while ago. Stephen and Rob rejoined the table now, and waited for their opportunity to speak with Bill.

195

I pulled my chair back a bit and sat trying to piece together all that had just happened. Without even a hint of the groveling I came prepared to do—without even the faintest word of apology!—this man, this old friend, had forgiven me simply because I was myself. There was nothing I could rationally do but forgive myself and move on.

"Ready to go?" George asked and received eager nods from Newt and Spunky and a tentative one from Betty.

"Is there anything else you want to do?" she asked me.

"Just one thing," I said.

She watched as I headed over to Eric Clapton. When I reminded Eric who I was, he perfunctorily extended his hand, muttered something polite, and stared as blankly as I thought he would.

"I've never told you how much I admire you," I said confidently. "You are one of the most talented musicians I've ever seen."

He nodded his thanks and I went off to rejoin Betty who had witnessed it all. We said our good-byes and our thank yous, and after exchanging a few phone numbers, exited.

As we waited for our car to arrive, I saw something small move in the shadows. I craned my neck to get a better look and there, still trying not to be noticed, stood Lisa Marie. She avoided my eyes and looked quickly around for her driver or some friend, but finding neither she stepped back into the shadows until she was almost completely in the dark.

I left the party feeling good. I had made my appearance, and I was hopeful about my future.

9

The Clock

Junkies get very close to their veins. Some are fearless favorites that never scar or abscess no matter how many times a day you use them or how dirty or dull the needle. Others are timid and playful and have to be treated gently and with respect or they become as fragile as wet tissue paper or simply disappear altogether. I once knew an old hippie who thought so much of a finicky foot vein that he named it Mary. He washed it four times a day, always wore comfortable shoes, and after a particularly good high through her, would go out and buy her some new socks.

"Got to treat her right," he'd say. "Never take a friend like that for granted."

I, of course, took everything for granted and at the end could shoot up only through my neck veins. If I'd listened to that old hippie, maybe I could have avoided the hepatitis that finally did my liver in, and I certainly could have avoided my fear and loathing of phlebotomists. Even when I was thin and white the best of them would run teary-eyed from my room, humbled both by their failure to find any blood in me and by my screams of outrage at their failure. Now that I'm bloated and yellow the task is impossible and so when the physicians finally judge me rational and well enough to unbind my hands, everyone politely asks that I take great care not to remove, entangle , or otherwise disturb my IVs. They also ask that I try not to talk just yet because my throat will still be too sore from the respirator tube that they just removed.

I am doing "remarkably well" and showing "no signs of rejection" according to the staff and they ask that I just lie still and heal. The moment I am free, however, I reach for the chalkboard near the bed and scribble on it the only thing in my mind.

"*Pain*," I whisper the word as I write it.

"Another ten minutes," the nurse says.

My doctors tell me that they will move me from the ICU to a regular room today if everything continues to go well. They show me a bag full of brown liquid and another one hanging on the other side of the bed that is filled with white, and a third full of a bloody fluid and say that these show that everything is working. They show me my "Williams Window," which is a red hole below my sternum the size of an almond and tell me that if I want to I can look in and see my insides. I shake my head no, and am about to whisper "Why the fuck didn't you sew that up?" when someone explains that it's open in case anything happens. "If you go into rejection then we can get a piece of your liver and find out exactly what's going wrong."

I react with horror and Dr. Makowka puts his hand on mine. "A very small piece. Just big enough for the micro-scope," he says. He is a big, thick, smiling man. Since the surgery two days ago he is always here, either with his team or alone, and I think his wife must hate me. Most doctors can't stand junkies, ex-junkies, and alcoholics. They see us as whining, weak, and self-indulgent, pissing on everything that they hold dear. In dozens of clinics and emergency rooms, after accidents and overdoses and suicide attempts, I've encountered their covert or overt contempt, but he has none at all. He treats me with a kindness and concern that I feel I do not deserve and so even though the pain is almost unbearable, this time I will not complain. During the next eight minutes and thirty-three seconds, I will lie there silently, my IV-impaled hands kept safely at my sides.

I stare at the clock. It is the same plain, unadorned, industrial clock that you find in schools and courtrooms. It makes me think of my life in increments of time. Forty-two years old. Sober five years. Two days out of surgery. Fifty-three minutes and eleven seconds since my last pain medication.

I watch the second hand jerk slowly forward and think about everywhere my mind has wandered in these last two days. When I began all of this, I promised myself that I would concentrate only on the future, but this has not happened. Something in me keeps flipping through the past in whatever direction it wants and, while I am increasingly convinced that this is somehow connected to my will to live, the clues are confusing and the possibility that death is in control is very real. The rational, optimistic side of me is very small and barely five years old. This side knows that my chances are good, that my pain is real and that my need for the morphine is genuine. The fatalistic side of me, large and dark and loud and thirty-seven years old, is convinced that I should have taken out a monster life-insurance policy for Betty and that I should be prepared to be launched into hell at any second. This part of me is convinced that my pain is minor and that my obsession with the morphine and the damned clock is just proof that I am still riddled with disease. The optimistic side wins for the moment as I think that my shrink will surely interpret this constant feeling of being under water as floating in amniotic fluid.

The team finishes work and they exit smiling. Enough time has passed so they are confident that there were no surgical errors: no nicks or tears, no slipped stitches, no sign of infection. Rejection can still begin at any second but my numbers continue to improve and tonight they will leave the hospital at a normal hour.

The room is quiet and empty and I wonder where Betty is. If she were smart she'd be at home and getting her first sleep in days but more than likely she's outside coordinating visitors. Darlene and my daughter, Sharlotte, are coming and as I comb my hair with my fingers, I notice that they're less swollen than this morning, almost back to their normal size. The itching has stopped, my skin is softer and less yellow, and my thinking is quicker. This new liver, this gift from some unknown boy, is strong and determined, and it has sent out new roots.

Someone appears at the door and I look up and see Stephen Stills and his son, Christopher.

"You're doing great," he says, cheerfully, looking at all my tubing and machinery. "Betty got us in. Told them we were family. She told me to tell you she's going home to take care of a few things and that she'll be back in a couple of hours."

I smile, thinking about how far we've come and how he *is* my family. My throat is too sore to say this so I point to my neck and he nods and pats me on the arm and changes the subject. Stephen starts talking about how big Christopher, now a teenager, has gotten and starts saying all the things that parents say to playfully embarrass their kids.

I listen and nod and try to stay in the moment but can't and I am seeing Stephen as I first did more than twenty years ago. He is thin and blond and looks like he was probably captain of the high school football team. John Sebastian has arranged this meeting and when we are introduced Stephen is polite but distracted and he shrugs me off. I set up my drums and waited for Stephen for quite a long time. He finally shows up, and we play terrifically for most of the night. In the morning he disappears without even saying goodbye.

We were soon a team—I was part of CSN, I was part of it all. Somehow this no-talent piece of shit had lucked into this incredible situation. When I first joined the band, CSN had just recorded "Suite Judy Blue Eyes" in Hollywood while I was still in New York working with John Sebastian. I overdubbed the drums on that song, which was hard because the tempo kept speeding up and slowing down. I think I was the first drummer to overdub on an already recorded track.

We worked at Wally Heider Studios in the heart of Hollywood and we would spend hours, even days inside. There were no windows and no clocks on the walls and there was no way of telling whether it was day or night—it was like being suspended in another dimension. Sometimes we'd stagger out exhausted and open the door to streets alive with people all dressed up and going to parties and clubs. But sometimes we'd open the door and the intense sun would hit us like a spotlight. I'd feel like a vampire, squinting and shielding my eyes the whole ride home.

It was four AM and we'd been trying to record David's song "Déjà Vu" all night. David was getting frustrated and I was getting tired; "take ten," "take twenty," and it still wasn't working. David laid down on the couch to rest for a few minutes while Stephen and I worked on the arrangement. It was David's best song and it had to be right. Suddenly David got up and strapped on his guitar for the final shot of the night and everything came together. They stacked vocals on it with renewed energy. We finished at two PM that afternoon.

The scenes are now coming fast and blurred. In each Stephen is brash, self-assured, unpredictable, and yet somehow, warmer. He shows me a vulnerable side he shows few people and gradually turns into a competitive yet protective big brother. He drags me along to most of his jams and introduces me to famous people. I think of the night we were scheduled to jam at The Scene in New York. We were just starting out, had no money, and we were crashing on David Geffen's floor. Sometime during the day of the jam we heard that Jimi Hendrix and Johnny Winter were also scheduled to play and we both got very nervous. Ahmet Ertegun, the head of Atlantic Records and one of Stephen's major fans, called and told Stephen he'd be in the audience that night, which made us even more nervous. To calm down, we started drinking heavily in the afternoon and by the time we were supposed to go on we were both too drunk to stand. When the show began Stephen sat on the stage while he played and I kept missing my drums. The audience was horrified but we continued to play, oblivious to them and to each other. So many times we did that. Perhaps if we had paid attention — to the audience, to critics, to friendly advice — my career would not have ended as it did and his would be even more accomplished.

Today beside my hospital bed Stephen is talking about his new songs and he is enthusiastic but cautious. The thin, athletic boy with menacing volatility and cocky self-assurance is gone, and before me stands a man who is funny and self-deprecating and aging as one should: with insight and acceptance.

As he smiles and laughs and coughs and I can see him laughing and coughing while he sat in the snow with his guitar and a red toy giraffe while the photographer took the cover shot for his first solo album. It was my first job after I got fired from CSN. Colorado was cold and the money wasn't very good, but he'd given me another chance and we were never closer.

I try to laugh, too, but I must look pathetic because he looks worried. Then I recall that I saw that same look the night he fired me for the last time. We had been touring almost nonstop with Manassas and were making some of the best music we ever made, but I had been getting deeper and deeper into drugs and Stephen had insisted that I go into, and in fact paid for, a drug detox program. A month later I returned a sober man and in less than a day I scored some coke, located an old rig, and shot up in a bathroom that no one ever used. Consumed by my first high in a month, I was too distracted to clean up after myself and as I was leaving the room to join the others, Stephen appeared at the door. Expressionless, he walked past me into the bathroom and for what seemed a very long time, he stood looking down at the white sink glistening with my fresh blood. I was silent. I offered no excuse and waited for his anger but instead when he turned toward me he was crying. He was worried and in pain and he hugged me and I cried with him, knowing that I'd crossed a line and that now he was every bit as lost to me as my mother.

We had only sporadic, bitter interactions for the next ten years. In the past year I had made some attempts at rekindling our friendship but he remained cool and skeptical. I had forged new friendships with David and Graham and felt accepted and respected by them and I longed for a chance with Stephen. But he kept me at a distance until I got sick and when he heard I was ill, the walls melted and I was given my chance.

Stephen talks of this and that—polite and clever conversation meant to distract. I want to ask him why we did all the things to each other that we did but my throat hurts too much, and of course the question has no meaning. Whatever it is that binds us together is also the thing that drives us apart and perhaps, someday I'll come to understand the psychology behind it all, but I prefer to leave it alone now.

The ten minutes have finally elapsed and a nurse appears and fills my IV with pain medication. Stephen waits uncomfortably for her to finish and then looks eager to leave. He has a dazed, anxious look that I have seen often in friends these past six months. It is the look of a deer caught in headlights; of a child looking into a parent's coffin, and I have grown accustomed to provoking it. This fear on their faces comforts me because it reminds me that I am not alone. I may exit this world first and soon, but everyone else will not be far behind.

I close my eyes, giving him permission to go, and he hugs me carefully and leaves with his son. The morphine begins to quiet all of the interior static and I breathe deeply with my newly freed lungs. I wait for sleep and the flood of dreams but it doesn't come and I take this as further proof that my new liver is thriving. I feel terrific until I look back up at the clock. Without sleep the hour is sixty minutes long rather than ten and with Betty and the transplant team gone there is a very real chance that the next person I see will be the meds nurse, fifty minutes from now.

THE CLOCK

Taking great care not to dislodge my IV, I reach for my blue notebook and the pen on the table next to the bed, and then arrange some pillows on my lap below my drains to use as a writing desk. I turn to the place that I left off when I got the telephone call that set all of the last few days in motion. This was the last chapter in the book I'd been working on for over two years. I'd made dozens of false starts, and had settled only on one thing: at the top of the white page, printed in large block letters, was the word *ACCEPTANCE*. I put my pen on the line just below it waiting for the familiar paralysis, but instead the pen takes off across the page.

I write for what seems like a long time and when Betty returns, I stop. I won't let her read what I've written and try to reassure her that I'm really working on the book and not a will, but she's still uncomfortable. When she leaves I pick up the notebook and write through most of the night. The details of the CSN&Y reunion concert are still fresh and vivid, and writing them down allows me to relive each moment. As I write I am amazed at how perfect an ending it is to my imperfect life and actually feel lucky. Few people have lived as much as quickly as I have and far fewer have been allowed perspective, as well as another chance. The reunion concert brought my previous life full circle and the transplant has allowed me to start a new one from scratch. The end of the book will be the first chapter of my new life; a life in which loss and betrayal will be recognized as a normal part of living, and will be met with acceptance rather than anger and despair.

In the morning I'm transferred out of the ICU to a regular room. There are many visitors and phone calls and my new life is beginning filled with love and support. I am tired but invigorated by hope. I have never felt so much for my friends; I cannot see my kids without crying; and when my sister tells me she is heading home to Phoenix, for the first time in my life I am genuinely sad to see her go. Betty watches all of this and is surprised as well as a little scared. She's been prepared for the post-surgical mood swings and steroid-induced depression that the team warned us about and so does not know what to make of this. I reassure her again but she's skeptical and again asks permission to read what I'm writing.

"We're out of the woods. Clear sailing ahead. No storms on the horizon," I say, amazed at how clichéd my speech has become.

"When do I get to see it?" she asks again, pointing to the notebook. She loves me but has her family's lawyer blood in her veins and can accept nothing at face value.

"In the morning, when it's done," I say, pulling her toward me. We kiss and when she leaves I open the book and write through most of the night.

10

The Reunion

Betty arrives early bringing new floral arrangements and cards and fruit baskets. She tells me of all the telephone calls on the answering machine last night leaving get-well wishes. Steve Perry has a cold so isn't allowed to come visit. Rob Lowe is out of town but sends his love and a fruit basket. Crosby is sending a bodyguard for crowd control. It is a warm day and the phlebotomist has just left with her samples but the results will not be in for a few hours yet. I am tired and know it's from lack of sleep so I don't tell Betty this. She sits on the edge of the bed and rubs her hands expectantly.

"So. Anything good to read around here?" she asks, looking around for my notebook.

"Some nice get-well cards from my nieces over there," I say, suddenly aware that my sore throat is feeling much worse. She gives me a sly smile and starts searching under the covers and pillows for the notebook, which I'm sitting on. She threatens to tickle me and I give it to her and tell her to

---

read it out loud. She opens the book and squints at my bad penmanship.

Betty was beside me, holding my hand, and on either side of us, my kids, Sharlotte and Dallas. Sharlotte was relaxed and beautiful and Dallas was anxious and looking too much like me. I was feeling tired and scared but more excited than at any time I could remember. Tonight was the answer to years of hard work and prayers and I opened all of my senses to take everything in.

The concert had sold out immediately and the auditorium was filled with yuppie aficionados, rock critics, industry types, and scattered old, stoned hippies who either had an "in" at the box office or who had donated a fair amount of money to the cause. All of the proceeds were to go to increase organ donor awareness in California and to help defray medical costs for those lucky enough to be recipients. Californians are notoriously stingy with their body parts and in addition, transplants are unbelievably expensive, as Betty and I had discovered when we found out that I would need a new liver. Never one to sit around and wait for things to change, Betty decided to do something about this, and with the help and advice of her mother and the devotion of Graham's wife, Susan, and Stephen's manager, David Bender, they established a Charitable Foundation to Increase Transplant Awareness to help offset the costs for recipients. Rob Lowe had started things off with a generous contribution and dozens of old and new friends followed suit with donations of their time or talent or influence. Tonight's concert at the Santa Monica Civic Auditorium was the first money-making event for the Foundation as well as the first time I would play with CSN&Y in twenty years.

Chris Hillman, whom I knew from Manassas, would start the evening off with his Desert Rose Band and then Don Henley would follow. After intermission, Neil would start off the second half as a solo act, and he'd be followed by Stephen and David and Graham. They'd play together, then each would do a solo number, then Neil would join the three of them onstage for a few songs and then I would join the four of them. The song we were to play together, "Wooden Ships," was suited to my physical frailty and couldn't have been more perfect in its symbolism.

The night was warm and the auditorium was loud and stuffy. I was constantly surrounded by friends and strangers coming up to shake my hand. The stage was black and bare, except for the instruments and the two enormous stacks of speakers. Long before the lights even started to dim the familiar smell of pot smoke drifted past me riding on gusts of warm, heavy air. The first time I had played this auditorium it had been warm and sticky like this. It was in the midsixties, and I was with my band Clear Light on a bill with Electric Flag and, I think, Iron Butterfly. We were all young bands, hoping that the right review or the right record company executive would pluck us from obscurity and make us headliners. That was the only thing that mattered, then. And this room was a lucky one; it was always a lucky one.

Despite all the preparations for the concert and for the surgery that was in my future, until the last two weeks some part of me had remained stuck in denial that anything was really wrong. But my deterioration had at last become obvious even to me. The beeper on my belt that would notify me when my turn came, almost overnight metamorphosed from an object of fear to one of hope.

This last week had felt very long—filled with as much practice and publicity as I could tolerate. I was tired all of the time now, with slower reflexes and a new forgetfulness that sometimes left me confused and lost on the freeway or midsentence in a newspaper interview. The sound check and rehearsal earlier in the day had gone well, at least Stephen and Graham told me it did, but I felt sluggish and was confused by something new they were doing in the middle of the song. I caught on well enough to fake it but was worried now that I wouldn't be able to remember what I'd done.

As I sat in the audience before the show, the crowd behind me was becoming impatient and entire sections were expressing their discontent by clapping their hands in unison. Chris was set up but he was nowhere in sight and I fought off the urge to go backstage to see what was going on. I wanted to be both observer and participant tonight and I knew it could be hard to find that balance and enjoy the moment, rather than long for another that was never meant to be. After rehearsal this afternoon, when everyone had gone, I had wandered behind stage and it was exciting to find my name on a dressing room door and invigorating to fill my nostrils with the musty smell of the thick, dark curtains. The lights and the rigging and the empty velvet seats stretching out before me brought back thousands of memories of being on tour and I longed for that experience again. Like a new amputee just becoming aware of the absence of a limb, I suddenly ached for that part of myself that was missing. Regret and longing were too familiar and powerful to allow in now and I did not want my enjoyment diminished in any way, so I headed for the door. I would go backstage briefly at intermission and then just before I went on to play.

Now total strangers were patting me, taking my picture or asking for my autograph whenever I turned around. The whole month had been like this: interviews with the *L.A. Times* and *People* magazine and *Entertainment Tonight* and a half-dozen radio shows. Phone calls and letters from misplaced old friends. Gifts and attention from the powerful and famous. The cocktail party at the Loews Hotel an hour ago had been filled with celebrities eager to lend their support and photographers eager to record it for their magazine or newspaper. With as wise and dignified an expression as I could muster, I hugged and kissed and posed as naturally as a Kennedy, while jumping up and down inside like a five year old at Disneyland. It had been a very long time since it had been like this, and it felt very good. The past four weeks had been filled with the attention and acceptance I'd been craving for years and while I was initially put off by the "Make-A-Wish Foundation" implications, I quickly dispensed with that. I sincerely believed that this was a beginning, not an end.

The lights dimmed. Chris and the Desert Rose Band walked on stage and the applause started. I hadn't heard Chris with this band but had played with him so many times and known him so long that I knew what to expect. Chris is an honest, multitalented man who, like me, had a penchant for acquiring wives. He had been with us in Manassas from the beginning and, while he could play rock & roll as good or better than the rest of us, his heart was rooted in country and he felt more at home with bands like his Flying Burrito Brothers. His audience had always been limited because of this, and instead of a superstar he became a musician's musician, known for a quiet, steady, and solid body of work. He opened now with sharp vocals and familiar harmonies, and expertly went through a tight set.

As the lights went up, the roadies started clearing the stage. Darlene poked me on the back and complained that her seats were too close to the speakers. Eric Gardner, my new manager who was sitting in front of me, turned and started talking excitedly about the first draft of the book and some changes that he felt were necessary. Kris Kristofferson, a few seats away from me, looked healthier than I'd ever seen him. Betty put her arm around me.

"Tired?" she asked.

"Nervous," I said. My arms and hands ached from all of the recent practice and the muscles in my neck were tight and sore. Drew Barrymore peeked from behind the curtain and waved. She was a longtime friend who, along with Judd Nelson, had volunteered to introduce the acts. Betty massaged my arm and waved for the two of us.

Don Henley's stage set was simple and stylish with stools for himself, his guitar players, and his backup singers, a grand piano, and a row of chairs for a small string section located at the back. As his people finished setting up, I thought of how surprised I had been when he offered to play because our interactions in the past had been brief and superficial. Betty, Judd, and I had sat in the first row during his rehearsal yesterday, and when his acoustic check was done I walked up on stage and thanked him. I told him what a fan I was of his songs and he responded by telling me how much I had meant to him when he was starting out on the drums.

"We drummers have to stick together," he said.

I invited him over for a quick look at the new drums given to me by Drum Workshop. He sat down and played and agreed they were great and we then headed back to the other side of the stage. When we shook hands I felt compelled to confess that I thought "Desperado" was one of the all-time great rock songs. He blushed appreciatively and I rejoined Betty and Judd for the rest of his set.

The lights dimmed as the three lithe backup singers took their stools, followed by the rest of the band. Then Henley was announced and he walked center stage, dressed in simple black and white, looking like a cowboy preacher. He sat on a stool, adjusted his microphone, and after a few words, went immediately to work. The audience fell silent, he closed his eyes and the piano sounded the familiar first chords of "The End of the Innocence." Plaintive, agile, and slightly frayed at the edges from wear, his voice led the group through a flawless rendition of the song.

I had heard this same voice years ago, coming from a boy in a new band whose strongest influence was CSN&Y. Of the legions of imitators only the Eagles had the talent to survive and surpass us. I could see Stephen and David watching from behind the curtain at the edge of the stage, hidden from the audience, and I could read envy and a certain amount of awe on their faces. They had never had Henley's level of success at going solo. Their songs lacked his power and edge, and their voices were now thin, finicky, and unreliable, in sharp contrast to Henley's seasoned, confident obedience.

I peeked over my shoulder and saw a sea of faces captivated by Henley's voice and the images and memories he evoked. I thought of my own life and losses and growth, and images of my innocent days floated by.

Betty stops reading because the nurse who is taking my blood pressure, pulse, and temperature seems distracted by the results.

"Everything all right?" I ask as the nurse writes her findings in my chart.

"A little high," she says, cautiously.

"Which one?" Betty asks, putting the book down.

"All of them," the nurse says as she starts to leave. "I'll be back in a little while."

"Do you feel all right?" Betty asks me.

"I stayed up too late. That's all it is," I say. "Keep reading." She looks at me for a moment before she does.

Henley finished his set without an error and the crowd went wild. As he began his encore I worried that everyone had come to see him, not me or CSN&Y, and I wondered how I'd feel and play if everyone left during intermission. This fear, combined with the smell of grass and my increasing exhaustion, caused a light-headedness and suddenly there was no keeping my eyes open. I laid my head on Betty's shoulder and watched as Don's roadies took their places behind the curtains and behind the walls of speakers, runners standing at their marks waiting anxiously for the gun. They would soon pick up and pack up, erase every trace of Don from here and carry him safely to the next horizon. Kind, efficient, faceless friends, they would take care of everything, freeing Henley of the trivial concerns of normal lives. "I need roadies again," I thought, and when I closed my eyes they were there.

They found me sitting in the grass behind the stage with Kathy and said that we'd be on in five minutes. I told them I'd be right there and asked Kathy if she wanted to come. She said, yes, and then we all headed out.

The roadies pushed and parted the crowd, and people strained to see who we were. Like always, I put my head down pretending that I didn't want to be recognized, but it was really to avoid looks of disappointment when they didn't recognize me. But I knew that someday I would keep my head up and see other things on their faces. As cameras flashed in our eyes, Kathy began taking pictures of the people watching us pass. As we got closer to the stage, I felt the nervousness rise.

I tried filling my mind with other performances to try to convince myself that this one was no different. I thought of the years with Clear Light and of playing with John Sebastian on his albums and of all the hundreds of times we played for rock's heaviest critics and stars at Stephen's house in Laurel Canyon.

More cameras were snapping and flashing as we walked and I really needed a drink. I thought, I'm too amped. . . . I'll get out there and blow the speakers, cover all the harmonies and lose my job. . . . Stephen would find another drummer in a second, it's all business to him.

As we got closer to the stage I grabbed one of the roadies and told him to find me a bottle of wine. He gave me a look as if to say it's not a good idea, but I yelled at him to do it now or his fucking job was over. At that, he took off to get it and the feeling of power momentarily took away my nervousness.

The back of the stage was more crowded than it had been all night. I could hear whispering as we pushed through, and I thought I heard my name. The crowd became even thicker and the edging through even slower when we reached the inside ring. It was filled with faces from album covers and magazines, all waiting for us.

They were waiting to see where we would take them. They were waiting because they knew that even if we weren't as technically sharp as we could be, the message and the feeling were going to change rock & roll forever. I looked over and saw Kathy standing at my drums clicking away at everything including the roadie waiting angrily with my bottle of wine. Then I turned away from the million impatient anonymous eyes facing the front of the stage to the thousand famous ones patiently watching my every move. David and Stephen and Graham were not on stage yet, Neil was hiding in the shadows behind a speaker and I was all they had to look at. So I grabbed the wine trying to look cool and nonchalant but the swig was way too big and the red liquid gushed out of my mouth and onto my shirt. I immediately did it again, trying to convince everyone that it was planned. I waved to Kathy to take a picture but something over my shoulder attracted her lens and I turned to see David coming onto the stage. He was rubbing his hands to warm them and talking seriously with a roadie. Hungry, important eyes were all over him but he ignored them and stayed completely focused on whatever the roadie was saying. Then Graham joined David on stage. He was drinking something from a cup and trying to act as casual as David about his stardom, but then he stole a glance at the crowd behind the stage and for a second, appeared nervous. Neither David nor Graham looked over to me and I sank a bit, feeling like everyone saw them avoiding me.

Then Kathy was next to me, very angry with herself because she hadn't paced her photographs and had run out of film. So I asked a roadie to take her to find some. They left and I was completely alone sitting at my drums. I sat with my head down, trying not to look behind me, trying to think only of the future. At moments like these the past always tried to get in but I knew I could fight it—I had to. If I didn't, I'd get sad and then I'd need some coke to pick me up and there was no time for that, so I focused on our next project—the second album—and concentrated on controlling my thoughts. Usually I was good at that, but this time it worked only for a second and then I was engulfed by an image of my mother. She was sitting at a table, looking young and pretty, drinking from a glass and watching me as Herbie and the men at the bar watched her. I took a deep swig of the wine and shook the image away and thought of all the women I was going to be able to ball after this concert.

I thought, "We'll be legends after tonight; we'll be rich and I'll have my pick of any woman I want. . . . Maybe I'll ball Ann Margret because she's got such great tits but I won't tell anyone because she's definitely not cool. After that maybe Grace Slick, then maybe Katherine Ross. . . . Yeah, driving on the Pacific Coast Highway in a Ferrari with Katherine Ross. . . ." She had her hand on my leg and I felt pleased and peaceful when suddenly the image dissolved and one of my mother replaced it.

I did not panic but I was getting frightened because I could not control what I was thinking or feeling, and I wondered if I had gotten hold of some acid somewhere today. That must be the reason, I thought, and I made a mental note to avoid acid in the future before performances.

I steeled myself against the rush of hallucinations to come and concentrated: The only memories I want are the ones I'm going to create from this point on and they are all going to be good. . . . I am going to play so well tonight that people will be talking about it for years and I'm going to be more famous than Keith Moon or Ringo Starr. . . . I'm going to wow audiences everywhere we go and I'm going to have my name on the front of the next album and I'm going to play with these guys as long as I want and when I've outgrown them in a year or so after a couple more gold albums, I'm going to start my own band that's going to play real rock & roll and we'll be bigger than the Beatles and everyone is going to know who I am and want to be my friend or be me and my kids are going to grow up rich and famous and never have to go through the shit I did.

Then my mood took an abrupt swing, and the bright images stopped. I thought of my kids back in California somewhere with their mother and I realized that maybe I'd already done to them what my father did to me. So I took another long drink of the wine and told a short roadie to find me a joint because this bad trip was definitely going to bum me out so much that it would affect my playing. While I waited, I looked up into the audience. Their faces were dimly lit, and so numerous and uniform they resembled a moonlit pebble beach. I waited for the acid to transform them, to alter their shapes, but when that didn't happen I realized I hadn't swallowed any acid, that these images from the past were real and something else was causing them to slip in. Maybe some new kind of drug, some anti-hippie drug created by Washington to bum us out — or maybe I'm just too damned sober. The idea of it being a plot hatched by Nixon was comforting, and I thought of writing a song about this new drug that sobers us up, turns us into our parents and dooms us to repeat their mistakes. I'd call it "Nixon's New Chemical Warfare" and it would have three drum solos and not one three-part harmony. The thought made me laugh and I felt good again and the roadie arrived with the joint. I grabbed it and smoked it hungrily, but I still couldn't shake the thought that I wanted to look up and see my mother sitting in the crowd. I never had stage fright when she was in the audience. I always knew that no matter how bad I looked or sounded, she would be there at the end of the show, proud and happy and clapping so softly I could hear her only after everyone else had stopped.

Then Stephen walked on stage. He was smiling and trying to appear as comfortable as Graham and David but he looked like I felt, and the thought occurred to me that maybe there really was some weird poison circulating and that we were specifically targeted. I got scared because I knew that I was definitely more creative and sharp when loaded on coke, and so was Stephen, and if that edge was taken away by some Republican plot then the future of rock & roll and maybe even the Western world would be in jeopardy. I thought that it must be because of "Wooden Ships" and that the people we were trying to change were trying to change us first and I wondered if I should tell Chip Monck to announce this to the audience, to warn them about the reality drug. I decided to check this out further and realized that the only logical course of action was to see if I could counteract the effect with more drugs. So I took a very long hit off the joint and then another and another and I almost fell over onto my drums. But I got caught midfall by someone standing behind me. I turned and saw a hippie with a dark beard and a ponytail wearing army fatigues and a T-shirt with a huge peace symbol on it. He was older, and when he smiled I could see broken teeth and when he stood back I saw that he had only one arm.

"Thanks, man. I think I've been drugged. You've got great reflexes."

"Not good enough," he said, pointing to his empty sleeve. I passed him the joint and got a closer look at him while he took a hit. From all the flags and peace symbols on his jacket, I figured he had to be a Vietnam vet.

"Wow," he said, holding the pot in his lungs.

"Unusually good shit," I agreed, taking back the joint. I was feeling very stoned and hopeful but then I started to wonder if he was a hallucination, too. "Vietnam?" I asked,

223

pointing to his arm. He merely nodded, waiting for his lungs to absorb every last particle of his hit. I slowly put my hand out and touched his jacket to see if he was real; he was. He laughed.

"I ain't no ghost," he said in a southern accent. "I travel with 'em. Eat, sleep, and die with 'em every night, but I ain't one yet." He patted me on the shoulder and then walked back into the crowd of critics and stars. He was gone. I felt very stoned and calm but in the distance, at the edge of the warm fog enshrouding me, I felt that something important had just happened. A political and angry feeling rose within me and I imagined that the faces in the audience were the faces of the servicemen over there, sitting in rice paddies and in foxholes, waiting for us to rescue them. I wanted to do something to prevent anyone else being maimed or killed. I thought, the only thing I can do for them is play and pray that the songs we sing and write will topple the government and stop the killing. And with this thought I filled with fire and ached to play. Stephen picked up his guitar and started tuning up.

The air had cooled. There was a slight wind and I could smell wet clothing and smoke. The crowd was eager to hear us and love us; the world was screaming for us to change it and I knew we could do no wrong. This was our moment, this was our planet.

Kathy was back and she stood watching me from the side of the stage. Her camera was hanging from her neck, forgotten for now because something had told her that she had to experience this moment fully, and not waste it by trying to capture it. I thought, She is so young and pretty, I want to be with her forever in this moment.

My hands were holding my drumsticks and they felt warm and ready and my skin was sweaty and tingling. The seconds before the music starts are always the richest, the most filled with possibility and electricity. Even though everything was already in slow motion because of the drugs and the audience, I wished that something would be invented or discovered to slow this moment down. I thought, If we can walk on the moon then surely some day we'll be able to stop time . . . hell, in our new world, there won't be anything we can't do. . . . We'll stop the war and feed the hungry, clean up pollution, cure cancer, and definitely learn how to tolerate people's differences. I thought of my friend Walter, who died because of the length of his hair, and knew that in our Family of Man, this would never happen again.

A camera flashed and its sudden light startled me and I realized that this was a new line of thought for me, none of this stuff sounded like me. What had happened to me since we arrived? What had changed me? Was this actually the Dawn of a New Day?

I looked up and saw John weaving in and out of the stage crowd, talking, laughing, and looking more excited than we were. When he got to me he hugged me and messed up my hair like I was his kid brother, and then he moved on. I thought about how much I liked him and hoped that when I was as old as he that I'd be as smart and write the way he does. As I watched him walking, the lights reflected off his glasses and somehow he reminded me of that astronaut who walked on the moon.

As the stage darkened, Stephen came over to me and looked into my eyes. At first I thought he was looking to see how stoned I was but then I realized that he was just excited and scared. I realized how much I liked him and wanted to be like him and how badly I needed his respect. Tonight, I vowed, I'm going to play like no one ever has before . . . and then they'll all crowd around me after the show and tell me they're going to put my name and picture on the front of the album with the rest of theirs. . . . Crosby, Stills, Nash, Young and Taylor.

Graham and David stood whispering, waiting for Stephen to join them so we could be introduced. Stephen took his place with them and all the stage lights went down and the crowd got quieter. The wind picked up slightly but I was warmer than ever and dying to play. The tarp above our heads was billowing and snapping and Kathy was crossing her fingers and everything was alright.

Stephen and David and Graham walked to the center of the stage in the dark and waited to be introduced. The applause started and swelled and I burned with the moment. This moment filled me to bursting. They started singing and it all began.

11

The Circle Closes

Betty stops reading because the team has arrived. I tell
her to continue because the good part is coming, but all of her
attention is focused on Dr. Makowka. He looks paler than
usual, and unhappy. When he opens his mouth he says the
word that we've been dreading and it's hard to take in. He
talks about this morning's blood tests and my fever and high
blood pressure.

"This often happens," he says, "and of course, we're
concerned, but all it means is that we have to go to another
line of drugs." Betty swallows hard and starts blinking a lot. I
sit perfectly still.

"You've had a great recovery, Dallas," he says. "You're
in good shape, you've got a terrific attitude, there's no reason
why you won't continue doing well."

"So bring out the big guns," I say. He tells me there is a
chance that this line of drugs won't work and I tell him I know
it will, so let's get on with it. He leaves with most of the team to

make arrangements to transfer me back to ICU because these drugs can have some dangerous, even lethal side effects and I'll need to be watched closely for the first twenty-four hours. A couple of his staff stay to tell me about the OKT-3 that I'll be on, or "Okie-Dokie," as they liked to call it.

The one thing that was certain about this medication was that it would make me very sick. OKT-3 is literally a poison made from mouse urine. The theory is that all of my T-cells would race off to neutralize it, thereby leaving my new liver alone. By the time they got back, that liver would just be part of the scene, like any old organ, and they'd no longer reject it.

Now Betty stands and begins to prepare for the move, gathering the few things that I'll need in a small bag. Her strength is remarkable and the look on her face suddenly reminds me of photographs of faces I'd seen in a book about Ellis Island, people not frightened by pain or the unknown, people who cope and continue.

I am just as resolved. This rejection cannot kill me. Rejection never has before. It's come damn fucking close but I pulled myself out five years ago and I'm going to do it again. I will survive this. I have survived an unprecedented number of close calls. I have survived an unthinkable number of sadistic medical tests and procedures and have no plans of pissing it all away just because some dumb fucking white blood cells insist on acting like nightclub bouncers too stupid to know they're throwing out the owner of the club. No, it does not end here. I will not let it.

They wheel me back to the ICU and as they reattach me to the monitors and machines, Pat, the head nurse of the transplant team, tells me in her calm and maternal voice that I will feel pretty shitty for the next few days and she pats me apologetically. She is a good and kind woman and like Dr. Makowka she's taking all of this very personally. Before she leaves I try to comfort her with a determined look.

Betty sits beside me as they put the OKT-3 into my IV bag and we watch the lines as it drips into my hand. She holds my other hand and chats about the fruit basket that Rob sent and the tropical floral arrangement that the nurses at work chipped in on. She knows these things really cannot distract me but she talks anyway. I flash back on other times I've had to will myself to keep living; other times that I have accidentally or purposefully injected a potentially lethal dose of something into these same veins and managed to keep all systems going until help arrived. This time would be no different.

We sit and wait for something to happen and when nothing does at first, the team is encouraged. They remind me that if I get past this rejection, and then the first year, my chances of living a "normal life span" are "good." I am considering what "good" means when something starts to go wrong. The aching in my joints and muscles doubles and the room fills with a light fog. I can see and hear and I feel Betty at my side but slowly everyone is starting to blur. I can focus if I concentrate hard enough, but even when I can get a clear image, I'm not sure if it's real or a dream. I try to relax and remember what it was like to be on acid and the importance of thinking good thoughts to avoid a bad trip. I try to take slow, even breaths but can't tell if I'm actually breathing or pretending that I am. The thought occurs to me that I might be dead already but when I concentrate and focus on the doctors, I see that while they have moved closer and are checking my monitors, no one is pounding on my chest, or even appears excited. I lie back and try to concentrate on the battle that's waging inside against my renegade white cells and I try to communicate to them, to tell them to get with the fucking program.

The fog gets thicker and thinking is much harder and I feel like I'm stuck in a plastic bag but I resist panic and hope that unconsciousness will come soon—but it doesn't. I am caught between sleep and consciousness and am part of neither world. This may be madness or limbo or hell but my instinct says to just hold on for the ride.

The darkness is filled with images that race by with great speed. I see Jimi brooding and Janis laughing and Cass Elliot sneering and rolling her eyes at me like she did so many times in Laurel Canyon. Then I see a friendly face and it's Gary Kelgrin, he's roaming the halls of the Record Plant with his mimosa, sucking on his bottle of nitrous oxide, and offering me a hit of something new and wild. But I can't keep up and he enters the water and drifts under, smiling.

Then Jim Morrison is there, knocking on the door of Stephen's house, telling me he's going to be a drug addict in a movie, he needs to get into the part, he needs an ounce of cocaine. We slide backward to an earlier time and we are standing in a parking lot outside a recording studio, trading swigs from a fifth of Jack Daniels. It's three in the morning and the Doors and Clear Light have each just finished some studio work, and Jim is showing me his new car. It's a blue 1966 Shelby Cobra GT Mustang 2 + 2 with a white racing stripe. I'm saying, "Nice fucking car, man," over and over. Then Jim jumps in, saying, "See you in hell, man," and he floors it, spins a donut in the middle of Sunset and races into the darkness down the wrong side of the street. "That fucker wants to die!" I yell, running away.

I feel something touching my forehead. I am back.

"It's OK," Dr. Makowka says, "You're out of the woods, the rejection is over."

I don't know how long I've been lying here, but I feel good. Somehow, even the forest of equipment makes me feel safe and warm.

Betty's hand is now stroking my cheek. In her other hand is my notebook and I want to ask how long has she been standing here, how long has she been clutching that note-book, has it been hours, days? But I don't; instead I smile at her and say, "Why don't you read it to me, honey? Don't you want to see how it ends?"

I was only halfway back to my seat when Neil took the stage and started singing. The lights hadn't even dimmed yet and he just walked on without an introduction, looking as worn and tattered as a street person. He played alone, with only his guitar, wandering the stage recklessly, fearlessly, and the applause was loud and long after each song. I watched David and Stephen standing behind the stage curtain during Neil's set and I worried—anything could happen. But Stephen looked calm which was a good sign. Then Neil got off and the roadies began loading the stage for the CSN set.

That's when I got too nervous to sit in the audience. It's hard enough to be in crowds but tonight made it even worse, so I stood up and made my way toward the backstage en-trance. I expected to be pegged at once by the security guard with a "Where do you think you're going, buddy?", or at least a "May I help you?" But he merely smiled as he opened the door for me, and I was half-surprised until I remembered, "Oh, yeah, this is a benefit concert for me!"

Then David, Stephen, and Graham were onstage, stand-ing in front of their microphones and the music began and

every note was where it should be. The old magic was back—
CSN sounded better than ever. Their harmonies were sharp
and clear and I thought, These guys really are the best.
Stephen was hitting notes he hadn't hit in years.

Once backstage I started to relax. I was really beginning
to enjoy the fact that this was all for me and I started
wandering around, just remembering what it was like to be on
the road with them. They would always start out acoustically.
All the electric guitars and the keyboards and stuff would be
on a large rolling platform, hidden behind big black curtains.
Then the curtains would part and the drums, et al, would roll
magically forward. It was an awesome sight.

My reverie was suddenly ended when I nearly collided
head on with a large man, who turned out to be a larger than
usual Jack Nicholson. I stuck out my hand and said, "Hi, I'm
Dallas Taylor and this is my party."

Taking my hand, Jack smiled at me, looking alarmingly
like the Joker. He shook my hand and in that nasal voice said,
"Very nice to meet you. . . . How are you feeling?"

We started walking together around the backstage area,
talking about how crowds make us nervous and then, every
once in a while it would hit me who I was with and I'd get star
struck and tongue-tied. I even asked a photographer to take
our picture together, which was completely out of character
for me—it was definitely not cool. But that night none of that
mattered, least of all being cool. All I wanted was to fully
enjoy every moment.

As we chatted I found myself thinking, Really nice guy.
Then I thought, Jesus! there's that word again, *nice*. It was a
new word to me and I'd been using it a lot lately, but it still
kind of stuck in my throat. I'd always avoided being *nice*. Nice
is downright limp-wristed: Nice guys finish last; it's not cool to

be nice. It's funny, Jim Morrison was really nice when he was sober; drunk, he turned into this raving maniac, very much like me—in fact, like most rock & rollers I've met, with few exceptions.

CSN&Y had come together and finished their set. Now it was the second encore and I knew it was time but it was hard to tell if this was a dream or reality. People were patting me on the back and saying things like, "Knock 'em dead, Dallas," or, "You're the best." But I'd forgotten how to play the drums and I was terrified. What if I fucked up? What if people laughed? What if no one applauded when they announced my name? Then I felt Graham's hand on my shoulder. I looked into his eyes and saw a love and compassion I had never noticed or thought was there, and I knew that this was my friend, my brother.

Graham pulled me by the hand onto the stage as the crew rolled a massive set of drums into the lights. And I could see that huge crowd, not one person had left; they were waiting for me. As the spotlight hit my face they went nuts. The cheers were deafening. They were on their feet.

As I made my way toward the drums, Neil came up and placed his hand on my shoulder and I could see Stephen, David, and Graham standing at their microphones, applauding madly, grinning from ear to ear. I sat down behind my drums and Stephen started counting off "Wooden Ships."

And it was as if we had been playing together this whole time, as if the last twenty years were a nightmare from which I awoke to find myself safe in my own room. Remorse, anger, and fear of death were gone, and I knew that everything would be all right.

We had come full circle.

Epilogue

Dear Betty,

Most books end on an up note. But considering the story I've been lucky enough to tell and your indispensable role in it, I can't think of anything more appropriate than to finish with a love note.

The Dallas Taylor I wrote about in this book would never have known a Betty Wyman, a beautiful, intelligent, thoughtful, sensitive kid from the ritzy hills of Bel Air. Our friendship, born as I surfaced from the depths of detox, was as improbable as our falling in love. Do you remember what you said when I started to show interest in you?

"Not interested. Too complicated."

You were right. Here I was, an ex-addict, broke, bored, and suffering from the blahs. You were from a family whose name was synonymous with L.A. politics and society. But we became friends, and then late one night I let myself into your apartment. You walked out of the bathroom in time to see me dump my clothes across the floor.

"Don't get excited," I said. "I'm not here to stay."

If addicts know how to do one thing, it's lie. We celebrated our fifth wedding anniversary on October 1. Do you believe it?

If this is a dream, I don't want it to end. Four months after the operation, I went on a 1,500-mile motorcycle ride from Los Angeles to Reno. On returning, my new liver was still where it was supposed to be, still functioning, and I never felt better.

At the six-month mark, doctors told me I had a seventy-five percent chance of seeing a year. And if I lived a year, then I would more than likely make five years.

Well, honey, it's been three years so far, and there's nothing but open road and blue sky ahead of us.

So far, so good. Today, in no small measure thanks to you, I live a full, fruitful, and productive life. I lead up to half a dozen drug and alcohol recovery and therapy groups, and I also play more music, and perhaps play it better, than ever before.

Just before my transplant operation, I remember Crosby saying that I'd gone through so many crises—sleeping in the gutter, stabbing myself, drug addiction—that I was destined to have one more miracle in my life. Of course, he was speculating about the surgery. But that was purely science.

The real miracle in my life was, and always will be, you.

Love,

Dallas

Fromin's Delicatessen
Santa Monica, California
October 12, 1993

Index

A
Alcoholism, 45
Alice Cooper, 180
Ann Margaret, 221
Atlantic Records, 19

B
Baez, Joan, 23, 144
Band, The, 23
Barrymore, Drew, 216
Beatles, The, 52–53
Bender, David, 212
Berry, Bruce, 50
Berry, Chuck, 12
Brady Bunch, The, 131, 135
Buffalo Springfield, 9
Byrds, The, 9, 92

C
Canned Heat, 23
Cantu, Mercedes, 46
Cars, discovery of, 83–84
Clapton, Eric, 175, 180–184, 196
Clear Light, 48, 232
  music of, 17
  performance and, 213
  playing with, 219
Cocaine, 34–35
  abuse of, 125
  CSN and, 20

effects of, 8, 49
  introduction to, 47
  looking for, 97–99
Cocker, Joe, 94, 181
Codependency, 120
Cohen, Herbie, 12–13, 221
Collins, Judy, 52, 88
Creedence Clearwater Revival, 23
Crosby, David, 9, 17, 18, 211, 238
  CSN and, 102
  CSN reunion concert, 213, 217, 220, 226,
    233–235
  Dallas Taylor and, 206
  "Déjà Vu" and, 203–204
  Joni Mitchell and, 192
  manner of, 91–92
  Woodstock and, 94, 101
Crosby, Stills, and Nash. *See* CSN
Crosby, Stills, Nash, and Young. *See* CSNY
CSN, 8, 13, 88, 128, 183, 203
  creation of, 17–18
  leadership of, 19, 20, 36
  leaving of, 162–163, 205
  money and, 22–23
  performance and, 9, 16
  reunion concert, 233–235
CSNY, 5, 52, 226
  breakup of, 125
  leaving of, 37, 38–40
  playing with, 235

CSNY *(continued)*
  reunion concert, 207, 212–218
  Woodstock and, 52, 95–96
Cyclosporins, 173

D
Daltrey, Roger, 87, 94, 96–97
Déjà Vu (album), 35, 39
"Déjà Vu" (song), 203
Derek and the Dominoes, 175
Desert Rose Band, 213, 215
"Desperado," 217
Diamond, Stan, 128–129
Dick Cavett Show, The, 87
Domino, Fats, 11
Doors, The, 22, 232
Drug rehab group, 111–125, 161–162
  Candy and, 66–70, 113–114, 136–147
  Christmas and, 136–147
  troubles in, 130–135
Drugs. *See also* Cocaine; Heroin
  abuse of, 42, 70, 125–126, 163–164
  acid, 221–222
  addiction to, 126–127
  attitudes about, 55
  CSN and, 23
  depression and, 166
  early use, 46–47
  experience and, 21
  hashish, 17
  leaving rehabilitation, 165–166
  marijuana, 46
  paranoia and, 141, 167
  rehabilitation and, 66–67, 72–80, 138, 205
  substance abuse counseling and, 152
  withdrawal from, 114, 118–121
Drums, 216
  attitudes about, 92–93
  grandmother and, 18
  lessons and, 12
Drum Workshop, 216

E
Eagles, The, 217
Ego, rock and roll and, 9
Electric Flag, 213
Elektra Records, 17
Elliot, Cass, 232
Elvira, 177
"End of the Innocence, The," 217
Ertegun, Ahmet, 19, 144, 204
Everly Brothers, The, 12
Experience, The, 22

F
Falk, Peter, 179
Fame, dealing with, 130
Flying Burrito Brothers, 215
Fricke, 11–12, 59, 86
  death of, 12
Friends
  death and, 26
  reunion with, 194, 206

G
Garcia, Jerry, 16, 90
Gardner, Eric, 174, 177, 216
Geffen, David, 52, 143, 182, 204
  CSN and, 18
  Laura Nyro and, 19
"Go Back Home," 184
Graham, Bill, 91
Groupies, 50–51, 187
  Laura and Lorna, 56
"Gypsy Eyes," 22

H
Harold and Maude, 184
Harrison, George, 181
Harrison, Patty, 182
Hendrix, Jimi, 100, 204, 232
  Denise and, 22
  Graham Nash and, 21–22
  music and, 183
  tapes of, 33–34
  Woodstock and, 88
Henley, Don, 213, 216–217
Hepatitis, 199
Heroin, 31–32, 73–74, 125
  junkies and, 199, 201
  overdose and, 41–42, 53–55
  use of, 49
"He's Not Heavy, He's My Brother," 7–8
Hillman, Chris, 128, 213, 215
Hollies, The, 7, 9

I
Ian, Janis, 87
Iron Butterfly, 213
It's a Wonderful Life, 112

J
Jagger, Mick, 126, 191
James, Rick, 33, 35
Jefferson Airplane, 23
Joplin, Janis, 33, 232
  Woodstock and, 23, 87, 105

K
Kane, Carol, 191
Kanter, Paul, 90
Kelgrin, Gary, 126, 232
Kesey, Ken, 117
Kristofferson, Kris, 216

L
"Lady of the Island," 21
Leary, Timothy, 177, 184, 185
Leonard, Sheldon, 116
Lifestyle
  responsibility and, 90
  rock and roll and, 8 – 9
  survival and, 140 – 141
  trouble and, 40
Little Richard, 11, 184, 195
"Love Gangster," 175
Lowe, Rob, 184, 195, 211, 212
  Betty Taylor and, 179
  reputation and, 186 – 187

M
McCartney, Paul, 125
McDonald, Joe, 15, 90
Mac Ray and the Invictas, 23 – 24
Makowka, Leonard, 29, 110 – 111, 200 – 201,
  229, 231 – 233
Manassas, 128, 163, 205, 213, 215
Married With Children, 184
Mayall, John, 180
Medical problems, 29 – 32, 65 – 66
  cirrhosis, 141
  liver and, 173 – 174
  liver transplant, 6 – 7, 109 – 110, 154, 202, 230
  medication and, 111
  pain and, 151, 158, 200
Miles, Buddy, 33
Mitchell, Joni, 87, 192 – 194
Monck, Chip, 60, 223
Moon, Keith, 89 – 90, 221
Morrison, Jim, 22, 232, 235
Music
  feeling of, 224 – 225
  importance of, 60 – 61
  influences on, 11
Music Minus One, 12

N
Nash, Graham, 142, 179, 191
  CSN, reunion concert, 213, 220, 226, 233,
    235
  Dallas Taylor and, 14, 206
  Jimi Hendrix and, 21 – 22

Joni Mitchell and, 192 – 193
  Laurie Sebastian and, 20 – 21
  manner of, 7 – 10
  music and, 102
  Woodstock and, 16 – 21, 96
Nash, Susan, 212
Nelson, Judd, 216
Nicholson, Jack, 234
Nyro, Laura, 19, 52

O
OKT-3, 230 – 231
Olympic Recording Studios, 180
One Flew Over the Cuckoo's Nest (Kesey), 117
Orbison, Roy, 11
Organ donor awareness, 212

P
Perry, Steve, 211
Presley, Elvis, 11
Presley, Lisa Marie, 178, 185, 192, 196

Q
Quaid, Dennis, 184

R
Record Plant, 126 – 127, 232
Recovery, friends and, 185
Reed, Donna, 120, 121
Richards, Keith, 98, 126
Rich, Buddy, 12
Roberts, Elliot, 18
Rock and Roll, 1958 and, 10 – 11
Rolling Stones, 176, 195
Ross, Diana, 133
Ross, Katherine, 221
Rothchild, Paul, 17
Rundgren, Todd, 177

S
Sag Harbor, 19
Sebastian, John, 13, 52 – 53, 91, 203
  cocaine and, 47
  CSN and, 20
  Dallas Taylor and, 17
  manner of, 14 – 15, 225
  music and, 219
  Woodstock and, 94
Sebastian, Laurie, 20
Segal, Katey, 184
Selleck, Tom, 131
Sex
  nature of, 115, 121 – 122
  Woodstock and, 15

241

Sha Na Na, 87
Simmons, Gene, 192
Sixties
  attitudes of, 40–41
  judgements about, 88
Slick, Grace, 87, 93, 221
Spector, Phil, 192
Starr, Ringo, 221
Steroids, 173
Steve Paul's Scene, 22
Stewart, Jimmy, 112, 116
Stills, Stephen, 23, 159, 184, 192, 195
  betrayal and, 125
  CSN and, 9, 17, 102
  CSN reunion concert, 213, 217, 219–220,
    223–226, 233, 235
  Dallas Taylor and, 18–19, 36–37, 128–129,
    205–206
  Eric Clapton and, 180
  hospital visit, 202–206
  leadership of CSN, 15
  manner of, 175
  music and, 33–35
  Woodstock and, 86, 88–90, 103
Stone, Chris, 126
Stray Cats, The, 177
Suicide
  Dallas Taylor and, 32
  drug rehab and, 68
"Suite Judy Blue Eyes," 203

T
Taylor, Betty, 186–187, 194–196, 208
  CSN reunion concert, 211–212, 216–218
  hospital visits, 83, 109–111, 173–174,
    229–233
  letter from Dallas, 237–238
  manner of, 151–153
Taylor, Dallas
  bands and, 23–26
  children of, 55, 202, 212
  control and, 123, 145, 169–170, 220–221
  Denise and, 22
  drug rehabilitation. See Drug rehab group;
    Drugs
  drugs and. See Drugs
  education, 21, 192–193
  family life, 55–56, 84–86, 160
  father and, 11, 58–59, 167–168
  financial problems, 128

guilt and, 56–57, 137, 144, 156
insecurities, 134
Kathy and, 93–106, 218–220
Laura and, 38, 163, 189
marriage and, 57
medical problems. See Medical problems
mother and, 155, 167–168, 221
mother and music, 11–13
mother's death, 24, 85–86
name and, 10
psychiatric help, 154–159
self image, 42
writing and, 207–208
Taylor, Darlene, 11, 45, 57–58, 202
Taylor, Mick, 126
Taylor, Nita, 55, 57–58
Tiffany, 179, 187
Townsend, Pete, 98
Trott, Thomas, 187

V
Ventures, The, 11, 12

W
Wally Heider Studios, 203
Who, The, 87
Williams Window, 200
Wilson, Brian, 70–71
Wings, 125
Winter, Johnny, 204
Winwood, Stevie, 181
"Wooden Ships," 213, 223, 235
Woodstock, 10
  CSN and, 91, 219–226
  experience of, 101
  groupies and, 48
  medical services at, 54
  people at, 60
  scene of, 15, 21, 47–48
Wyman, Astrid, 174–176, 180, 185–186,
    188–190
Wyman, Bill, 126, 174, 177, 195
  Dallas Taylor and, 188–190
  music and, 175–176

Y
Young, Neil, 213
  CSNY and, 37–39
  CSNY reunion concert, 233, 235
  music of, 102